FAITH UNDER FIRE

FAITH UNDER FIRE

Wellesley Muir

REVIEW AND HERALD® PUBLISHING ASSOCIATION
WASHINGTON, DC 20039-0555
HAGERSTOWN, MD 21740

Copyright © 1988 by
Review and Herald Publishing Association

This book was
Edited by Raymond H. Woolsey
Cover Design by Dennis Ferree
Cover Illustration by Mark Stutzman

Scripture quotations, unless otherwise indicated, are from the New King James Version. Copyright © 1979, 1980, 1982, Thomas Nelson, Inc., Publishers.

Texts credited to NIV are from the *Holy Bible, New International Version.* Copyright © 1973, 1978, International Bible Society. Used by permission of Zondervan Bible Publishers.

Printed in U.S.A.

R&H Cataloging Service

Muir, Wellesley, 1926-
  Faith under fire.

  1. Pinedo, Leonardo. 2. Seventh-day Adventists—Biography.
I. Title
                        922.6

ISBN: 0-8280-0495-1

SPANISH DICTIONARY

Abrazo A hug or embrace.

Adventista Adventist—a member of the Seventh-day Adventist Church.

Balsa Raft made from balsa logs.

Barbasco A poisonous root sold to chemical manufacturers; also used by Amazon Indians to poison fish.

Calabazo Dungeon or cell; a tiny prison cell with just enough room for a man to stand; sometimes a place of torture, where water is run over the prisoner's head.

Chonta A palm, the wood of which is elastic and harder than ebony.

Cinco Five.

Centavos Cents, but worth much less than a U.S. penny.

Fiesta Celebration.

Hermanos Brothers and sisters in the church.

Machete Cutlass or chopping-knife; it's the tool of the jungle.

Mamá Fond name for mother.

Mamita Especially fond name for mother; "dear little mother."

Papá Fond name for father.

Plaza City square, often like a park.

Santa Biblia Holy Bible.

Señor Sir or mister.

Señora Mrs.; title of respect for a married lady.

Señorita Miss, young single lady.

Soles Peruvian money—difficult to compare with dollars because of constantly changing exchange rates.

Yuca Casava—a stringy, starchy root grown in tropics and eaten like potatoes. It's a staple in the Amazon jungle.

CONTENTS

1. Illegitimate Son   11
2. Shoot on Sight   17
3. Stolen Bible   24
4. Flame of Love   33
5. Son of God   40
6. Swallowed by a Boa   48
7. Dreading the Draft   55
8. Sabbath in Uniform   62
9. High Jump   69
10. Flags at Half Mast   77
11. The Calaboose   86
12. Plump and Pretty   96
13. Gun Over the Heart   102
14. Witch Doctor Remembers   109
15. Legitimate at Last   117

Chapter 1

ILLEGITIMATE SON

They are unfaithful to the Lord; they give birth to illegitimate children. Hosea 5:7, NIV.

Moonlight filtered through dark branches of tall palms, bringing a magic glow to the jungle landscape. Only the crack and pop of flickering flames broke the silence of the Amazon night. Eager youth sitting on rough log benches around a campfire leaned forward in anticipation. Many of them were attending a Seventh-day Adventist youth camp for the first time in their lives. They were not prepared for what they were about to hear.

Flames leaped higher, lighting the face of a strong young man who stood to speak. Earlier that day they had watched him setting up camp. Tents had been provided for the campers, but there were no beds. This sturdy youth with well-developed muscles used a machete to cut raw materials right out of the Amazon rain forest. The grateful campers knew that this young man's expertise in jungle survival provided the beds they would sleep on that night.

They listened. Mouths dropped open as he finished his first few words. "My existence is the result of a lustful love affair by passionate youth. I'm an illegitimate son. Circumstances of my birth haunted me. I've stayed awake nights wondering why I was born like this. Could anything good ever happen to an illegitimate child? Could I become a true son?"

He struggled to remember what his mother had told him about his early years. He could only guess at some of the details.

* * *

No moon shown on the night young Adela lay screaming inside a palm-thatched hut. Rather, a storm raged, while piercing pain convulsed her body. Late in the evening her boyfriend, José, dropped by for a visit. He held her hand saying, "Everything will be all right."

She wanted to be comforted, but other thoughts jumped around in her head. *He thinks everything is all right. Why doesn't he marry me? I should have listened to the priest when he talked with the girls in our village about the seventh commandment. Worse than the pains I'm having is all this disgrace of bearing a baby without being married.*

Sometime after midnight, José left with Adela's mother to call a midwife. Adela groaned between pains. *Will no one come to help me? I want to shout, but how can anyone hear me with all the thunder and lightning of this tropical storm?*

Even then Adela's mother was stumbling through the darkness of the violent downpour. Unable to locate the midwife, she was returning alone. Wet clothing clung to her skin as she slipped and slid on the muddy path along the Ucayali, longest tributary of the great Amazon River.

She struggled to keep from falling down the steep bank into the swift river. She could see her way only when lightning flashed. A roar of thunder shook the ground as her feet touched the rough board steps that led to the hut. Hearing the cry of a newborn infant she exclaimed, "Oh, I'm too late for the delivery!"

Adela sobbed from her mat on the floor. "Is this just another miserable girl? You can throw her in the river. This is the fruit of my fornication. José will never marry me! I just want to die!"

Adela's mother lit a candle. "It's a boy," she almost shouted. At these words the new mother pulled herself up and looked into the face of her son. "I'll name him Leo-

ILLEGITIMATE SON

—Leonardo—'brave as a lion.' Anyone who grows up in this land of jaguars, crocodiles and big snakes will need to be very brave."

The rain stopped as long fingers of light streaked over the tropical green. "A boy!" Adela marveled. "Will José really care for me now so we can get married?"

Days later, town fathers at the remote Amazon village of Contamana issued a birth certificate: "Leo—the illegitimate son of José Pinedo and Adela Sánchez."

Adela, proud of her firstborn, moved in with José. Although they never married, they lived together long enough to have three children.

Before Leo's second birthday, ugly skin eruptions broke out all over his little body. The medicine his mother secured from the government medical outpost had no effect on the pussy, oozy mess. After weeks of searching for a cure, Adela heard words of defeat from the first-aid officer. "Sorry! I've tried everything. I can't help your baby."

The young mother shuffled slowly across the town plaza with Leo on her back. At a park bench, she untied the bundle and laid the boy down. Gently she pulled back the cloth covering his body. "This infection is awful. My son will die!" she cried aloud.

A woman strolling through the plaza saw tears on the young mother's cheek and stopped to look at the child. "Oh, how terrible! Haven't you heard about the witch doctor's cure?" she asked.

"The best medicine from the government first aid station hasn't worked. What could a witch doctor do? I've heard they charge a lot of money and cast spells. Maybe he'd blame me. What if he decides to kill me? I'll just pray a little harder to the Virgin Mary," Adela replied.

"If you want that boy to live, you'd better take him to Virgilio Izquierdo. True, he's killed a few people, but he's the best witch doctor in the whole upper Amazon jungle. And I hear he's very good at curing children's diseases," the stranger persisted.

Leo's mother eyed the woman. "Where is this witch doctor, anyway?"

"He lives about a day up river by canoe. Remember his name—Virgilio Izquierdo. Don't forget that name. He's a very proud man." The superstitious woman fingered a tooth charm and added, "I wish you all the luck of a magic crocodile tooth."

Adela hurried to find José. Early the next morning with little Leo in her arms, she followed his father to the river. They placed boiled yuca and ripe bananas in the bow of a dugout canoe. Mother and son sat in the middle and José took his place in the back. He reached for a paddle and pushed away from the bank; they began to move upstream. When the current became too swift, he steered the canoe close to the river edge and pushed forward with a long pole.

The warm Amazon sun hung low on the western horizon when they finally reached the witch doctor's hut at Tipishca. The cunning man sent word that they must wait. Adela turned to José in fear. "What if he blames me?" she asked. "It's not fair. You got me into this. We never should have had this child."

Long shadows from jungle trees reached over the clearing before the crafty spirit worshiper came out. "The sun is almost gone. Why did you come so late?" he asked as he pulled back the dirty cloth from Leo's festered body. "Ugh!" he grunted. "This is the worst I've seen." He stared at the mother and then the father. "Is this your wife?"

"Uh, uh, we're not married, but this is our son," José stammered.

The witch doctor started again. "This woman is to blame. Without her death, the boy should die. But if you pay my price—100 *soles* in Peruvian money—I'll pray to the spirits. They can teach me how to mix up the right medicine."

The frightened father agreed. "I'll pay your price." He counted out the money.

The witch doctor began to dance. He stretched his arms to the sky. He mumbled strange words. Finally as if under a spell from the spirits, Virgilio Izquierdo brought out a dirty bottle. He slowly stuffed it with pieces of tobacco leaves. He added camphor, alcohol, and some mysterious ingredients.

ILLEGITIMATE SON

He took the dying boy in his arms and continued his frenzied dancing. Then he stopped and placed the child on a table. He took the dirty bottle, held it to his lips and sucked in a big mouthful of its contents. He began spitting the strange liquid onto the oozing sores. After several big mouthfuls, he completely covered Leo's tiny body with the nasty concoction.

The trio spent the night under a mosquito net near the witch doctor's home. When morning came Virgilio Izquierdo advised, "Your son will get well soon. You better get going down the river before it gets too hot."

After settling down in the canoe José remarked, "I wonder if Leo will live to see the witch doctor again?"

Coincidence? Cure? Was it the magic of the witch doctor's medicine or the hand of Providence? The infection disappeared and the sores dried up. Adela rejoiced. *Leo will live—this boy who should never have been born! Could there be a reason?* she wondered.

As the boy grew older, playmates on the streets of Contamana taunted him with ugly names that sent him home crying.

"Mamita, why do the kids call me 'bastard?' Was it bad for me to be born?"

Adela tried to change the subject. "Leo, you were born on a very important day in our country—the eighteenth of January. Your birthday is on the anniversary of the founding of the Peruvian capital city of Lima."

The boy showed no interest in national holidays. He wanted his friends to call him "Leo," not "bastard."

Jose invited Adela to move with him to a new home on the Cachi Yacú River some two miles from Contamana. A Quechua Indian living in the jungle explained, "*Cachi* means salt and *yacú* means water." Leo's father began operating a small salt factory.

He diverted water from the river into large vats, which were heated by the tropical sun. The water evaporated, leaving a residue of salt. José collected and packed the salt in small baskets made from jungle plants. Vendors sold the salt on the streets of Contamana. Financial success made it possible to hire men for the work at the salt plant. José joined the new revolutionary political party and began spending almost all his time in politics.

Adela, with concern for her own future, questioned José. "Why don't you just take care of the salt business? We ought to get married and raise our children. Let the politicians worry about government."

After Leo turned 6, his father made the mistake of publicly criticizing the ideas of a popular leader. "You have no right to yield to clerical pressure. Your philosophy is all wrong," he said.

Immediately the man threatened, "You'll pay for this. The politicians of Contamana aren't going to accept any nonsense from you, Señor Pinedo! Just watch and see what happens."

Only a few days later, Leo and his sister, Guillermina, were home alone. Adela had taken their baby brother to Contamana, and José was out on an evening walk. Leo looked toward the salt factory and his heart skipped a beat.

"Guillermina, come!" he called. The children watched uniformed soldiers carrying rifles march right into the salt plant. Leo squeezed his sister's hand. "I think something terrible is about to happen."

The military men came with orders to kill José Pinedo and take over the factory. Returning home, José heard the commotion at the salt plant and rushed into the house. He grabbed his two frightened offspring and fled to a hiding spot under a clump of *chonta* palms.

The soldiers turned from the salt factory and headed for the house. The leader shouted, "Don't let him get away. Shoot to kill!" The men raised their guns and shot from every side, riddling the house with bullets.

Leo and Guillermina clung to their father crying, "We don't like this place. We want to go to Mamá. Won't the soldiers find us here under the palms? Oh, Papá, they'll come and kill us!"

Chapter 2

SHOOT ON SIGHT

They push the needy off the road, so that the poor of the land are forced to hide. Job 24:4.

"Sh!!!" José whispered as he turned to his son. "Leo, your mother gave you a great name: 'Leonardo—brave as a lion.' You need to be brave. If these soldiers ever find us, they'll fill our bodies with bullets. We've got to hide just like jungle animals and make sure we're never heard or seen. Do you understand? And you too, Guillermina!"

"But Papá," Leo pleaded. "We want Mamá. Why can't we go and stay with her?"

"I told you to be quiet!" José raised his voice more than he intended. "We've all got to be quiet right now!"

The soldiers, who had been sent by enemy politicians, began operating the salt plant. They kept hoping José Pinedo would appear so he could be assassinated. Any man who dared to criticize the corrupt leader must die.

Leo remained with his father and sister in the *chonta* palm hideout for several weeks. José managed to communicate with Adela. She already knew about the authorities intentions to destroy him.

José struggled to survive. "No way can I keep these children hidden under these palms forever. I can't go to their mother and I'm not going to let them go to her."

One night soldiers came so close that José heard their secret conversations. "The police and military in Contamana have their orders. When José Pinedo appears, shoot him on sight. And if he doesn't show up soon, we're to search him out and eliminate him."

The next morning José spoke softly to Leo and his sister. "We can't stay here any longer. They're out to get us. They're going to comb the jungle until they find us. While you were sleeping I made secret arrangements with an old friend. He gave me his dugout canoe. There's no moon tonight and no one will see us. We'll leave as soon as it gets dark. We must get across the river and make sure they never find us."

The father and two children had lived like nocturnal animals for weeks—sleeping in the day and sneaking out to find a little food at night. Leo should have spent the rest of the day sleeping. Instead, he spent it with anxious thoughts racing through his mind. *Why is Papá taking only Guillermina and me? Why doesn't he take my mother and our baby brother?*

There's no twilight in the Amazon jungle. When the sun goes down, darkness follows immediately. Father whispered, "We'd better be going. Guillermina, you walk right behind me. And Leo, you brave one, you walk along behind and make sure no one is following us."

Leo protested, "But Papá, I want Mamá to come with us."

"Be quiet, son! Don't say any more about that wretched woman. She's not my wife and we don't need her on this trip."

They took their few belongings and walked through the dark, dense rain forest so softly that even wild animals did not seem alerted by their presence. They reached the steep bank of the Ucayali and felt their way down to the water's edge. A canoe with three paddles awaited them. Leo took a paddle and went to the front. Guillermina sat in the middle.

Father took his place in the back. He whispered, "If we are going to make a quick getaway, everyone will have to paddle." He stood and stared out into the darkness in every direction. Not even the shadows moved. But then he thought, *There must be people around. There's always someone on the river. The soldiers can't be too far away.*

SHOOT ON SIGHT 19

José stepped back on the riverbank. He leaned forward and with a big shove leaped into the canoe. The tiny craft slipped silently out over the black water. Bright stars filled the Amazon sky and José kept asking himself, *Is it possible that there is enough light to make us visible and alert our enemies?*

The anxious father and his two small children paddled all night. They crossed the Ucayali and headed downstream. They were still paddling when a brilliant orange sun, climbing out over the tall green jungle trees, brought the mouth of the Cushabataya River into view. Guillermina cried and Leo almost lost his paddle when they saw a giant crocodile with ugly teeth stretched out on a sandbar in the early morning sun.

By continuing downstream they could have followed the Amazon all the way to the Atlantic Ocean. However, during the night, José finalized upon a different plan. He had grown up in another section of the Amazon. His aging mother still lived in the distant city of Juanjuí, in the state of San Martín. He thought, *I'll be safe by returning to the land of my youth. The presence of my two children will help keep me from being recognized as an outlaw.*

They were still in view of the crocodile when Leo yelled out, "Papá, what are we going to do?"

"We're going up the Cushabatayo River. We're going all the way. We're going as far as our little canoe will take us." José didn't mention that it would mean 18 tiring days on the water under the blistering Amazon sun. He just said, "Keep on paddling! We've got no time to waste."

Leo kept looking back to see if any soldiers were following them. All at once he straightened up and held his paddle out of the water. What's all the shouting? Are the soldiers catching up with us?"

José laughed. "That's just a bunch of howler monkeys out in the jungle. Don't worry. In the daytime, we'll see our enemies long before we hear them."

One day they hugged the edge of the river, trying to get around a series of dangerous rapids. Swift current caught the bow of the canoe and whirled them around, pushing them far out into the river. They were now headed back downstream straight into rapids they had tried to avoid. José saw the danger and shouted to his children, "Get down low and hang on!" A big wave swept over the bow and swamped the canoe. They hurried to rescue a couple of paddles that got away. All of their belongings would have been lost if José had not tied everything in securely.

On the eighteenth day they reached Varadero, a point where the river became impossible to navigate, even in a small canoe. José still feared being followed and he didn't want to be captured. *I've just got one choice*, he thought. *Keep on going!*

José spoke to Leo and Guillermina. "This is where we leave the canoe," he said. "From now on, we'll be walking." Ahead lay virgin jungle, a range of mountains, more jungle, and finally the Huallaga River. "When we get to the river, we can float to our destination in Juanjuí," José suggested.

The trip would have been difficult for an expedition carrying the best equipment. This father traveled with a 5- and a 6-year-old and practically nothing else. He did carry an old shotgun and a machete. He often cut into jungle vines to get drinking water. He used the gun for killing birds and small animals for food. Occasionally they found wild fruit.

They spent miserable nights trying to sleep in the rain forest without even a mosquito net to protect them. During the day they walked westward, through jungle so dense that José often had to cut away the undergrowth with his machete in order to continue.

Late one day José stopped as though he had just walked into a stone wall. He cried, "We're being followed by a jaguar." Leo and Guillermina raced up a tree like a couple of monkeys. Father followed to the base of the tree. The jaguar crept close.

José aimed his gun carefully, realizing that a shotgun is not made for killing large jungle cats. He knew of men who had been killed and eaten by jaguars. For once in his life he wanted to pray. He thought *Is this any better a way to die than to be killed by the soldiers I've been fleeing from? Adela was right. I should have married her, taken care of our children and stayed out of politics. There's no way to kill a jaguar with a bunch of buckshot.*

José shook as he placed his finger on the trigger. He fired one shot. The wounded jaguar roared and raced away through dense jungle vegetation. It took a long time for the frightened father to persuade his trembling offspring to climb down out of the tree.

Eighteen scary days up the Cushabataya River in a canoe and three months of torture walking westward in virgin jungle brought the trio to the bank of the Huallaga. "Papá, how are we going down this big river without a canoe?" Leo questioned.

"That will be easy," his father assured him. "We'll take our machete and cut a few balsa logs and tie them together with jungle vines."

They waited until the next day to board their newly made balsa raft. Guillermina could hardly believe her good fortune. "Papá, will Leo and I get to rest our feet all day?"

"Well, maybe not all day," father replied. In just a few hours they reached Juanjuí. Though his feet ached, José rejoiced. He had reached the home town of his youth. He would see his mother. There would be decent food. At last he felt safe from his political enemies.

Everything seemed strange to Leo and his sister, who wondered if they would ever see their mother again. She was three months and 18 days away. They were in the state of San Martín. She was in Loreto. The children's heartbreak grew when their father moved in with a mistress called Señora Leonor.

José took his children to see their grandmother. Leo felt from the beginning that he didn't like her. She lived in a big house where every room had several images of saints. It seemed she had a special saint for each week of the year. That's all she talked about.

Leo recalled that back home in Contamana he had attended Mass with his mother. *It's true*, he thought. *I saw some images, but I also heard the priest talking about God. Why doesn't anyone here in Juanjuí ever talk about God?*

Leo didn't like living at his grandmother's, and it was even worse with Señora Leonor. *Maybe she likes my father, but she sure doesn't like me*, he told himself.

José worked hard, bought land, and began farming. He planted lots of cotton and *barbasco*. *Barbasco* is a root used by Amazon Indians to catch fish. Products from this root were in demand by laboratories in Europe and America. With the sale of these crops, money came rolling in. José built up a good cash reserve and his home lacked no material thing.

Farming proved a total success for José. He talked with Leo and Guillermina. "You know, children, the day will come when you have no mother or father by your side."

Leo snapped, "I don't have a mother by my side now."

"That's not what I'm talking about, but you do have Señora Leonor." The father continued, "What I wanted to say, you are growing up and you must learn to work so you will know how to make a living when the time comes."

Leo enjoyed working, but he also loved to study. He found so much joy in reading books that he finished primary school by the time he was 11. José encouraged his son. "Leo, you've done well. I want you to become a lawyer."

Leo wondered, *What would my father think if he knew what's going on inside of me? What I really want is to learn about God. I want to learn about spiritual things. What makes me want to be good and bad all at the same time?*

No high school awaited Leo in remote Juanjuí. His father made friends with Tomás Pestañaz Aguirre, the kind parish priest from Spain. José took advantage of this friendship and arranged for his son to use the parish library.

Each Sunday Leo carried a big pack on his back, loaded with eggs, chickens, rice, peanuts, and fruit as a gift for the priest. In return he was allowed to enter the library and use the books. In two months he had read every book about St. Anthony; every issue of the magazine, *Osservatore Romano*, edited in the Vatican; and many other publications.

Leo's grandmother filled her house with images of saints. Now he read everything he could find to discover what the different saints were all about. It left him with an empty feeling. He thought, *There's got to be something that will give me satisfaction.*

Near the end of a Sunday afternoon in the library, Leo looked through a stack of old magazines. Suddenly he found something under the pile. He gasped, "I've never seen this before in all my life. The big book had a green leather cover. Printed in gold letters across the front were the words, Santa Biblia (Holy Bible). He picked it up and dusted it off. He discovered on the title page that it was the Catholic version of the Scriptures, by Bishop Felix Torres Amat, of Spain.

Leo read a few lines from Genesis. "In the beginning God. . . ." His heart seemed to accelerate. He read the rest of the chapter and reasoned, *God must have made everything, even the great Amazon jungle and me.* Never had he found such satisfaction from any other book.

He looked around. *I'm alone. No one else is in the library. The priest doesn't use this book. It's gathered dust for a long time. It will be easy to get out of here without being caught. I'm going to take this book home.*

Leo wrapped up the big green book, stuck it in his sack, and started to walk out.

Chapter 3

STOLEN BIBLE

You have known the Holy Scriptures, which are able to make you wise for salvation through faith which is in Christ Jesus. 2 Timothy 3:15.

Leo had never stolen anything in all his 12 years. Now a lump filled his throat, his mouth seemed dry, and he felt a burning sensation behind his ears. He trembled all the way out of the library. On the street he wondered, *Why is everyone looking at me? Will my friends find out I'm a thief? Will the priest check his library and discover the book missing?*

Every few steps Leo glanced over his shoulder, just to make sure no one was following. His legs felt like the gelatin dessert he'd eaten at the only restaurant with a kerosene refrigerator in the whole city of Juanjuí. Home never seemed so far away. "Whew!" he sighed, when at last he turned down the path that led to his house. "Sure glad I made it. No one must ever find out about this."

Señora Leonor sneered and turned the other way when Leo walked in the house. The stolen Bible was too big to hide under the mattress. He found a place under the bed where the book would be safe and out of sight. But placing the Bible where it couldn't be seen did not stop his anxiety. *What if Papá catches me with this book? He'll ask me where I got it. What am I going to tell him?* Leo went to bed early but it took him a long, long time to fall asleep.

José's farm prospered. He owned lots of cattle, fat hogs, fields of cotton, *barbasco*, sugar cane, and beautiful fruit trees. Sales of these products brought in an abundance of cash. The fact that José paid his children only five *centavos* a day had nothing to do with the farm's financial situation. He just wanted his children to learn the benefits of hard work without expecting to be paid large sums for all they did.

Financial success made it possible for José to hire more and more men to care for the farm. At last he found time to study books of law, which had always held an attraction for him. With more money and spare time, he involved himself in politics again. He tried to forget that involvement with politicians had caused him to lose his salt factory and everything else he owned back in Contamana.

Leo came home one afternoon and saw his father sitting alone in a chair. "Papá, you look so pale. What's the matter?"

"Don't know, Leo. I haven't felt good for several days. Today I feel terrible and I'm getting worried."

José spent the next several days in bed. He complained about being very uncomfortable and his mistress, Leonor Rengifo, paid him a great deal of attention. Leonor finally convinced him to see the local doctor. The family physician did all kinds of tests and had José return many times.

One day the doctor asked him to sit down. "Señor Pinedo, you're not going to like what I have to say."

"Go ahead, Doctor. You might as well tell me the truth now."

"After a careful diagnosis, I must report that you have cancer of the larynx. This will be difficult to cure, however you can be sure that I will give you the very best treatment possible. And there's one thing you can do. You'd better stop smoking."

"Cancer?" José's eyes flashed anger. "What you're really saying, Doctor, is that I'll probably die. Let me tell you, I've already smoked my last cigarette."

Early that night, Leo blew out the kerosene lamp by his bed. Apparently everyone believed he was sleeping. He overheard Leonor talking to his father. "You're a sick man and you will need me to take care of you for a long time. Your children are getting old enough to care for themselves. I want to stay and help you get well."

José listened without saying a word. His mistress continued: "We've lived together for almost six years. I think it's time for us to get married. There's just one thing. I don't want to see any more of Adela's children. They've got to go."

Leo could hardly wait for morning to come so he could tell his sister. Guillermina and Leo guessed that the woman their father lived with figured he would be dying soon. She would have to get rid of them and marry Leo in order to receive all of his estate. Anxiously they waited to find out what their father would do.

José made an immediate decision to separate from this calloused woman and keep his two children. He believed the successful farm operation insured sufficient money to take care of all their financial needs.

For the first time in their lives, the children felt that perhaps their father really loved them. Leo decided it was time to tell him about the stolen Bible.

"Papá, please don't whip me for this!"

"What have you done, Leo?"

"I stole a book—it's a big one."

José demanded to see it. He followed the boy into his bedroom and watched him drag a large green book from under the bed. Instead of scolding his son, the father smiled. "How about a deal? Let's work out a schedule so we both can read it. The Holy Bible! This is God's book. Years ago I learned about the Holy Scriptures, but I wasn't interested. Now I know this is the book we need in our home."

They made an agreement that allowed Leo to read the Bible during the day and his father would study it at night.

Money had been the last of their worries. Now José needed expensive medicine imported from Germany. They sold hogs and cattle. Thousands of *soles* came in, only to be spent for medicine. Papá's health improved, but the farm animals vanished.

The father and son continued to share the stolen Bible. Days passed and José spoke with Leo. "Son, this is the truth! This really is the Book of God. I've made an amazing discovery. The seventh-day is God's Holy Sabbath. Jesus made the world in six days and rested on the seventh. It's a special day of rest in honor of the Creator. From now on, no one in my house is going to work on Sabbath."

Leo read about the Sabbath too and agreed with his father. They discussed how to celebrate the holy Sabbath day. They continued studying, and for nearly a year tried to keep the Sabbath. José searched in encyclopedias and other books to get information about people who might worship on the Sabbath. He searched without success, except that he found another Bible like the one they were using; he bought it on the spot for cash.

Although Leo struggled to honor the Sabbath, his conscience kept reminding him of another commandment: "You shall not steal." He knew he must return the stolen Bible to the priest. Inexperience in taking things that didn't belong to him got him into trouble when he took the Bible back.

He wrapped the big book with the green leather cover in the same cloth he had used when he stole it the year before. Arriving at the library he started to carefully place the Bible under a stack of old magazines. He failed to notice that the priest, Tomás Prestañas Aguirre, entered the library behind him.

"Leo! Leonardo Pinedo!" The priest came close. "What have you been doing with this book?"

"Father," he addressed the priest, "I—I—I'm putting it back in it's place."

"But what are you doing with it? Have you read this book?"

"Yes, Father, I read it."

"How many pages have you read?"

"I read everything—all of it. I've read it from beginning to end." Leo imagined, *Surely the priest will be happy that I'm a good student—that I've taken time to read this important book from cover to cover.*

"Who else has read this book?" the priest demanded.

"My father read it too."

"You little fool! Don't you know that this book is not to be read? It will make a demon out of you." The angry man continued, "I don't read it because I don't want to become a demon. The Bible is here in my library like the tree of knowledge of good and evil in the Garden of Eden. With all the marvelous books in my library, why did you have to read this one?"

"Father Pestañaz, in this book I learned about the foundations of the heavens, how the world was created, the purity of Joseph. I read how God used Esther to save her people. I learned more about Jesus than I ever heard in all my life. Jesus died to save us from our sins. He wants us to love Him and keep His commandments. How can this book turn me into a demon?"

Leo spoke politely. "Thank you for being so kind in sharing your library. If it's a problem, I won't come any more. Please forgive me for taking the Bible home without getting your permission."

"Leo, if you are going to continue reading the Bible, I don't want to see you any more. You may go and not come back. Do you understand?"

A friendship of many years deteriorated. Leo felt bad and glad at the same time. At least he didn't have to feel guilty about having a stolen Bible in his possession.

Almost every town in the Amazon jungle has a pool hall with billiard tables. About the same time Leo started reading the stolen Bible, he began going to the pool hall. He found life complicated—he had a desire to serve Christ, but he also wanted to follow the ways of the world.

Leo was standing at a billiard table when a friend offered him a cigarette. The other man held a match and helped Leo light his cigarette.

From that hour on, every time Leo played billiards he had a cigarette hanging from the corner of his mouth. He thought himself a real man of the world.

Love for tobacco tempted Leo to a life of lust and vice. He had never experienced a conflict like this before. Even as he tried to walk the way of Satan, the Lord, through the Holy

STOLEN BIBLE

Spirit, reached out to try to save him. Leo read, "Let love be without hypocrisy. Abhor what is evil, Cling to what is good" (Rom. 12:9). He wondered, *When I know what's good, why do I lust for what's evil?*

The Bible he'd been reading reminded him, "Make no provision for the flesh, to fulfill its lusts" (Rom. 13:14).

José smelled tobacco on Leo's breath. He placed his hand on his son's shoulder and said, "Remember how I stopped smoking when the doctor discovered I had cancer of the larynx? Tobacco can produce many other harmful effects on the body. Son, I want you to stop smoking."

Without hesitation Leo looked his father in the eye. "I will never touch a cigarette again," he said. He made this promise not expecting to keep it, yet fully realizing that the Bible teaches, "Lying lips are an abomination to the Lord" (Prov. 12:22).

Fiesta time arrived in Juanjuí, with its days of celebration, drinking, and dancing. Before leaving for a club, José gave Leo money, suggesting that he go to a special dance for teenagers on the opposite side of town. Leo didn't have a lot of interest in the dance, but he thought, *Hey, this will be a great chance to get out of my father's sight and smoke.*

After arriving at the youth club, Leo crossed town again to check on his father. José seemed busy and Leo felt secure. He ran back across Juanjuí and found a dark corner in the club where teenagers danced. He sat down and pulled out a cigarette. He held it between his lips and lit up. Just as he started to inhale, a strong hand touched his shoulder. "Hi there, young fellow," said a voice. "You really know how to smoke."

Leo jumped up. It was his father. Leo trembled. The cigarette and match fell to the floor. A look of shame filled his flushed face. *I deserve to be slapped. My father will beat me and send me home,* he reflected.

But José just looked at Leo and spoke quietly, "You smoke like a real gentleman." After saying, "Good-bye now," he walked away.

The boy ran home. He cried bitterly because he knew he had deceived his father and lied to God. He dumped out all his tobacco and matches. "I will never smoke again," he vowed. He never put another cigarette in his mouth, he never touched marijuana or cocaine, and he never took one swallow of an alcoholic beverage.

Leo and José read the Bible and endeavored to keep the Sabbath. They even started setting aside tithe and offering, but they didn't know what to do with it. In spite of good intentions, they still lived more or less like the worldly people of their town.

Leo turned 14 about the time an evangelical missionary from England moved to Juanjuí. Leo's desire to associate with Christians led him to take part in Sunday school. He became uncomfortable when Rev. Cooper told the class that the law of God was nailed to the cross.

"Young people, when you're saved, it isn't necessary to worry about the law of God any more," the preacher said. "You can eat what you want. You can dance. You can have your little love affairs. It's all right to drink a little beer and wine. None of this is sin because we are not under the law but under grace."

Leo reported this to his father, who assured him that all this is contrary to the Word of God. "You know that I've lived a life of sin. I've lived with different women and I have illegitimate children. I've gotten into all kinds of vice and corruption. Jesus died on the cross to save us from all our past sin, not to give us permission to continue to sin. All the expensive medicine I buy to stay alive is a price I pay for a life of sin. Jesus wants to save us from our sins."

José directed his son to a number of texts that teach God's law is eternal. He then quoted Jesus' words: "Do not think that I came to destroy the Law or the Prophets. I did not come to destroy but to fulfill" (Matt. 5:17).

Leo wrote down all the texts his father read. At Sunday school the next week he raised his hand. "Could we clear up the questions about the law that were raised last week?" he asked.

Rev. Cooper replied, "We're not going to discuss this again." When Leo insisted on a reasonable answer, he was

STOLEN BIBLE 31

asked to leave. "I don't want to see you again," he was told. This ended Leo's relationship with that church.

Leo's sister, Guillermina, never became interested in the Bible. She ran with the boys in town and eventually ran away with one of them.

Leo worked with the hired hands running the farm.

In spite of poor health, José spent most of his time in politics. He received special honor when the governor for San Martín named him sub-prefect for the district of Juanjuí. This made him the highest political authority in the area. Many of the social functions he attended were totally out of harmony with God's Word.

On a Saturday when Leo was 17, his father approached him. "There must be some people somewhere who keep the Sabbath holy," he said. "I keep wondering if there are any here in Juanjuí."

They began a search that took them to the outskirts of the city. They stopped in front of a weather-beaten, thatched-roof hut. They heard voices of people inside, singing hymns. They looked and saw six people. They asked questions and learned that they were *Adventistas del Septimo Dia* (Seventh-day Adventists).

José asked, "Do you believe all the Bible and follow all of its teachings?" The humble folks answered with an enthusiastic, "Yes!"

The father turned to Leo. "*Adventistas*? This must be the religion we learned about in the priest's Bible. Here are people who keep the Sabbath."

José and Leo asked, "May we come and worship with you?"

Six faithful Adventistas, who had worshiped secretly for some time, rejoiced to have the highest political authority of Juanjuí join them for Sabbath worship.

José's political life required too much compromise with Bible standards. The Holy Spirit reached deep into his heart. He knew there was only one way to go. "I must follow Jesus. I will write to the governor and thank him for the honor of being appointed sub-prefect and ask him to accept my resignation."

Leo's father left the political scene completely in order to worship with six poor, uneducated Adventistas who worshiped on the seventh day under a thatched-roof hut they called a church. He told Leo, "It is better 'to suffer affliction with the people of God than to enjoy the passing pleasures of sin' [Heb. 11:25]".

Former friends hated José for his new religion. One Sabbath, father and son spent the entire day with the *hermanos Adventistas* (Adventist brothers). They even stayed for a special meeting in the evening.

But while José and Leo worshiped in the little hut on the edge of Juanjuí, enemies entered their comfortable home and carried off their clothing, furniture, tools—everything, including all the money they kept hidden in a large trunk. Finally these wicked men took the kerosene lamps and poured out the kerosene, allowing it to soak into the wooden floor. They threw lighted matches onto the kerosene and ran.

Chapter 4

FLAME OF LOVE

For whom the Lord loves He chastens, . . . But if you are without chastening, of which all have become partakers, then you are illegitimate and not sons. Heb. 12:6, 8.

The fire spread rapidly. The dry, wooden-framed building burned like a drum full of oil; flames climbed high into the evening sky.

About 9:00 p.m. Leo and his father left the Adventista meeting and walked toward their attractive home in the best part of the city. They stopped short on the path leading to the front door. "But where is the house? Could this be possible? No house!"

They saw only smoldering ashes. They soon learned that everything of value had been stolen. The house and what was left had been burned. Father and son stood speechless.

José broke the silence with words that impressed Leo. "Everything I've worked for all my life is gone and it doesn't matter. What they can't take is the flame of love that burns in my heart. I'm going to keep right on believing in Jesus."

Grandmother came, with some of Leo's aunts. She didn't come to show sympathy for the disaster or to offer help. "Now you see, don't you! All this happened because you joined a fanatical religious group. Now you can go to those little Adventista devils. They will give you all the help you need. Aren't Adventistas supposed to help Adventistas?"

"Huh! They're all so poor, they couldn't help a sick flea. They didn't even protect your property from those who came to ransack and burn. You should have had enough brains not to get mixed up with this foolish religion. Don't expect any help from us. We won't even give you a glass of water!" She walked away.

After spending the rest of the night with one of the *hermanos*, José and Leo decided to rent a house. They found one for only five soles a month. The owner wanted the rent in advance. But there was no way to make this payment, for the thieves had carried off the big trunk containing all their money before they had set fire to the house.

All the farm animals had been sold earlier to buy medicine. There was no money to pay for help to work the farm. Leo worried about his father's health. "I just don't see any way out of this situation," he complained.

A smile broke over José's face and he started quoting Job 21:1: "Naked I came from my mother's womb, and naked shall I return there. The Lord gave, and the Lord has taken away; blessed be the name of the Lord."

Leo looked for a job and found work with Sabbaths off. An engineer paid him two and a half soles a day for working Monday through Friday. It delighted Leo to be able to return his tithe, pay rent, and buy some food.

They managed for awhile, but without the costly medicine José's health grew worse. "Leo," he said, "I've decided it's time to move away from Juanjuí. My old friends stare at me. My relatives make fun of me. With my knowledge of the jungle, we could get along much better living up the Huallaga River."

Leo liked the idea of a new adventure and agreed to the plan. Father and son crossed the Huallaga and walked along the left bank for 15 days. José had to walk slowly because of his weakened condition. They spent nights under protective palms and lived off whatever food they could find. Sometimes they stayed two or three days in the same place, waiting for José's strength to increase.

Each night and morning they had family worship. They took turns reading precious passages from the Bible. Occasionally other travelers joined them and listened with interest to the reading of God's Word.

The Peruvian government made jungle land available to anyone who would occupy it, and José chose a spot near where the Cachi Yacú River entered the Huallaga. Leo asked, "Papá, are you choosing this site because it has the same name as the property where you had the salt factory when I was small boy?" Mention of the salt factory brought tears to the tired man's eyes.

"Things are different now, son. You're going to do all the work." Leo gathered material from the wild jungle and followed his father's instructions for putting up a two-room, thatched-roof hut. His dad showed him how to build excellent beds with native materials cut out of the jungle. They enjoyed the simple life, living off the products that could be found growing wild all around them. Time passed rapidly, spent in survival and in study of the Word.

They had learned many hymns at the little Adventista church in Juanjuí. Now they sang them over and over. Their favorite is found on page 313 of the old Spanish hymnal. It's No. 524 in the American *Seventh-day Adventist Hymnal*. The father-and-son duet echoed through the jungle as they sang it again and again:

> 'Tis so sweet to trust in Jesus,
> Just to take Him at His word:
> Just to rest upon His promise,
> Just to know, 'Thus saith the Lord.'
> Jesus, Jesus, how I trust Him;
> How I've proved Him o'er and o'er!
> Jesus, Jesus, precious Jesus!
> O for grace to trust Him more!
> —Louise Stead

Early one morning Leo walked four miles up the Huallaga River to get some eggs. He decided it would be fun to float back down the river. He straddled the trunk of a banana tree that he found floating, and discovered that it supported him. With his belt he tied his clothes and eggs around his neck. Using a stick, he paddled toward the center of the river, where the strong current picked him up and sped him along.

Leo didn't know that while he walked up river there had been a cloudburst on the headwaters of the Cachi Yacú. When he got to the place where the two rivers joined, he found the Cachi Yacú flooded. All its water poured into the Huallaga, pushing it back. The rivers rushed together like two giant bulls fighting each other.

The current picked up Leo on his banana trunk and swept him straight into a whirlpool. He screamed as it spun him around and sucked him into the center, in 30 feet of water. As he felt himself being drawn down deeper and deeper, he lost all hope of ever getting out. Thoughts of his father flooded his mind. *How will Father ever get along alone? Oh, Lord, Your will be done!*

Flashing in his mind were the Spanish words of that favorite hymn, "And I know that Thou art with me, wilt be with me till the end." It seemed like he was praying and singing and holding his breath at the same time. "Jesus, Jesus, how I trust Him."

When he least expected it, when he was sure he could hold his breath no longer, he was thrown out near the edge of the river. He grabbed desperately for some vines near the river bank and rested until he could get strength to walk on home.

José spent 14 months teaching Leo the secrets of jungle survival. He spoke quietly one evening as they sat by an open fire: "Son, we've lived in the jungle long enough. I'm not a savage. I've always lived like the upper class. I don't feel well. I want to go back and die in my home town. Please take me back to Juanjuí."

In the morning they read words from the Psalms and prayed for guidance. They decided to join the men on a large balsa raft that was floating down the river. In his weakened condition, José could hardly get out of bed. Leo saw that he had no energy at all. On the raft he fixed a special bed with palm branches for shade so that his sick father would suffer as little as possible.

In Juanjuí, one of the *hermanos Adventistas* offered them a vacant hut. Leo did his best to tenderly care for his failing father. On the third night, Papá called Leo to his side. He said, "Son, I'm going to die tonight. I'm not afraid of death. I know that Jesus will resurrect me at the time of His coming.

"There is one thing that makes me very sad. Because they stole my money and burned the house, I'm not able to leave you any inheritance. Because I failed to make you legally my son, you won't even get the land. All I can leave you is some advice. You must never separate yourself from the counsel of Jesus found in the Bible."

José reached out and gripped Leo's hand. "As you know, I've been a very wicked man; as part of that wickedness, you were born in illegitimacy. I've prayed and asked our precious Lord for forgiveness." His voice faltered. Words came slowly. "Leo, Jesus wants you to become a son of God."

Tears flowed down Leo's cheeks as he reached his arms around his father in a strong embrace. Suddenly his father's life was gone.

José Pinedo never had the privilege of meeting an Adventista pastor, yet his greatest desire had been to be baptized into the Seventh-day Adventist Church. Those who knew him, those who saw the changes in his life, those who felt his sincerity and inclination towards the things of God, knew that he had been baptized by the Holy Spirit. Like the thief on the cross, José had prayed, "Lord, remember me."

Leo cried over the death of his father. His Catholic grandmother came and said, "Leo, your father's dead now. It's time for you to forget all this Adventista foolishness. Bring your father's body to my house. We'll call his old friends, the doctors, the officials. They will all come. He's not a dog for you to take to that miserable hut that belongs to the Adventistas. If you do that, you can be sure that none of his family will come."

"Grandma, thank you for all your kindness," Leo replied, "but I just want to mourn with my Adventista *hermanos* tonight." The brethren came and wrapped José in a white sheet. Then very tenderly, they moved him to the Adventista chapel.

The group of six Adventistas had tripled in size since Leo and his father first found them. They helped Leo in every way. They were not allowed to use the city cemetery so they worked together to dig a grave on a jungle clearing and conducted a simple service. Grandmother and the aunts did go take a quick look at the body while it was still in the Adventista chapel, and then returned no more.

On the day following the burial, Leo's parish priest friend came by to reprimand him. "Your father was an important man in the city of Juanjuí. Why did you bury him like an animal? We could have rung church bells advising everyone of your father's death. He served as an important political authority. We could have celebrated a solemn mass permitting his soul to rest in peace on it's journey toward heaven."

Leo pursed his lips. "There's no such thing as a soul that leaves the body at death. If you can teach me from the Bible that the dead need something, I'm ready for mass to be said at this very moment. God extends grace to the living and not the dead."

"I knew this would happen to you!" the priest cried. "You read the Bible there in my library. You've been converted into a demon. You've never done anything worthwhile! Good day!" he snapped and walked away.

Leo had missed his mother for 12 years. Now with father gone, he felt more lonely than ever. A relative came to console him. "Too bad, Leo, that your father didn't leave an inheritance of a house and money. But you know, there is a little land and it ought to be farmed. You can't work it by yourself. What you really ought to do is fall in love with some pretty señorita and get married."

Leo mused, *Father made no will, and with my illegitimate status it will be difficult to get the land. But a pretty señorita, someone for me to love—I like that idea!*

When he met Anita, whose flashing eyes hid behind long dark eyelashes, emotions seemed to flood every part of his being. He spent more and more time with her. He almost forgot about the group of Adventistas out on the edge of town who had been so kind to him after the loss of his father.

Love? Lust? Leo knew he had to have Anita. The two agreed they would ask her parents for permission to marry.

Leo rehearsed the words he would say and approached Anita's mother and father with a happy heart. They showed tremendous resistance. Finally the girl's father looked straight at him and said, "Look, boy, the answer is No! You're a young man without an inheritance. You don't have anything to offer. You can never be a good husband for our daughter. She deserves something better than a bastard."

Leo felt his world crumble. *Anita's folks think I'm just an illegitimate orphan. Guess it's true. The priest told me that I've never done anything worthwhile.*

He staggered to a park bench in the city *plaza*. His heart ached as he sat down in an effort to recover. *It's not my fault the way I was born. Why does everyone have to bring it up?*

He jumped when a warm hand touched his. It was Anita. Unnoticed, she had come and sat close to him. "I've got the solution to our problem. It's true my parents don't like you. My uncles don't like you either. Don't worry. It doesn't matter. Let's go to some far off place. Let's go live in the jungle. My parent's are always trying to control my life. I've got to get away. My heart's on fire. Take me anywhere you want—I'm ready." Anita spoke with passion. "Leo, I love you! Let's run away together!"

Chapter 5

SON OF GOD

For as many as are led by the Spirit of God, these are the sons of God. . . . The Spirit Himself bears witness with our spirit that we are children of God, and if children, the heirs—heirs of God and joint heirs with Christ. Rom. 8:14, 16, 17.

Leo searched Anita's lovely dark eyes. "Run away? We'd be crazy! To travel on the river, we'd have to carry our things in waterproof bags. And with millions of mosquitos, you might get malaria. To try and cut our way through virgin jungle would be worse. When I was 6 my father took my sister and me 18 days fighting rapids up the Cushabataya River in a dugout canoe. Then we spent three terrible months cutting through dense jungle. I don't think you want to live with crocodiles and jaguars, Anita."

Still, the suggestion made by relatives that he should get married troubled Leo. *Perhaps Anita's idea of living together without getting married could work*, he considered. He saw her many times in secret. They finalized plans to run away the next Tuesday. *Why not*, he thought. *I took care of my father for fourteen months in wild jungle. I can make a jungle home for Anita.*

Airplanes seldom land in the remote Amazon area of Juanjuí. When one did come, everyone ran to the airstrip to join the excitement. Just before noon on Monday, Leo stood with the crowd as a CAMSA DC-3 plane touched down and taxied to the rustic terminal. He watched an attractive woman with a beautiful smile and one gold tooth walk down the ramp.

Youth from the little Adventista chapel surrounded her, and Leo joined them. He nudged a friend. "Who is this woman?" he asked. His friend replied, "Her name is Señora Mercedes Guerra de López. She's the wife of Pastor Esteben López."

Leo asked, "Señora, why have you come to Juanjuí?"

"I'm just here on a short stopover. I wrote several youth inviting them to come to a youth congress this coming weekend in Tarapoto. I want to make sure they're going to come. I'd like to have you come too!"

Leo had never met a woman who seemed so kind, so courteous, so loving, and so motherly in dealing with youth. She learned that his father had died recently and she called him aside. She certainly seemed to understand that his life had been filled with a great deal of anguish.

She asked, "Do you have a problem that would keep you from going to youth congress?"

"I have many problems, Señora."

"Would you like to tell me about them," she continued.

"Oh, just a lot of personal things that I don't need to bother anyone else with."

"Do you have financial problems?"

Leo didn't want to tell her that he had no money at all. He stood there without answering her question.

Señora López didn't give up on Leo. "Do you have family problems?"

"I can thank the Lord that I have no family problems. The only one for whom I've been responsible is resting in the grave."

"Do you have any social problems?" And with a twinkle in her eye she added, "Maybe you have a girlfriend. Do you have an Adventista girlfriend that you don't want to leave while you go to the youth congress?"

"No!" He hesitated, then added, "My girlfriend is not an Adventista."

She looked squarely at Leo. "Do you know that the Bible teaches, 'Do not be unequally yoked together with unbelievers? You certainly won't want to have a courtship and marriage with a girl who is not a Christian."

Leo responded, "I think I read that verse one time."

"Do you think you could be happy with someone who is not a Christian?"

"Well, eh, not necessarily. But she's the only girlfriend I've ever had. She's the only one who makes me happy."

"What are you thinking about doing? Are you planning to get married?"

"No, we have other plans."

Leo knew that this smiling lady with the gold tooth had touched his real problem. He intended to live with a girl out in the jungle without getting married. He and Anita would steal away at 3:00 a.m. the next morning. Anita had a good suitcase hidden from her parents. All their things were packed.

All kinds of thoughts flashed into Leo's brain. *Did God send this pastor's wife at the right time? Is the devil trying to get me to sell out for a life of lust? Do I really love Anita? If we carry out our plans tonight, I may never discover the joy of living a life of real love! God's word says, "Flee sexual immorality."*

Señora López spoke softly. "I suppose you don't have money to attend the youth congress."

"That's true. I don't have a single centavo."

She opened up her black purse and handed Leo several bills.

"This is too much!" He handed back part of the money.

"No, you keep everything. You may have some other need. Just promise that you will attend the youth congress."

Leo promised, just as all the "in transit" passengers were called to get back onto the plane.

His decision made, Leo spent the afternoon and evening preparing for a trip to Tarapoto. He had planned to meet Anita at 3:00 a.m. behind her parents' home for their runaway. Instead, at 2:00 a.m. he boarded a fragile balsa raft with a group of youth to float down the river to Terapoto to attend the youth congress. There had been no time to tell Anita, yet in his heart he felt he was doing the right thing.

It took two days to reach Tarapoto. Leo bought a pencil and notebook so he could write down everything he heard at the congress. At the opening meeting, missionary Stephen

SON OF GOD

Pritchard, president of the Upper Amazon Mission in Peru, challenged the youth with "Share Your Faith!"

Never before had Leo witnessed a meeting like this, with large numbers of youth attending. He knew he must share his faith too. All the emptiness he felt after losing his father seemed to vanish. The difficult decision to leave his girlfriend seemed insignificant. He felt transported by the Holy Spirit to the very doors of heaven.

Now was the time for action—time to preach—time to teach-time to talk with children—time to tell everyone that Jesus is coming soon. These thoughts seemed to take complete control of his life. He found the congress exciting and mind-consuming.

When Leo learned that there would be a baptism on the final day of the congress, he went to the mission president. "Pastor Pritchard, I want to be baptized!" he announced sincerely.

The pastor asked, "Young man, is there anyone here who can recommend you?"

Leo knew that even the youth who brought him on the raft really didn't know him, and they weren't baptized either. There wasn't anyone who could testify of his conversion.

Pastor Pritchard questioned, "Who gave you Bible studies and taught you doctrines?"

"No one, Pastor. I just studied the Bible for myself, but I've tried to keep the Sabbath for six years."

"My young brother, isn't there someone who can recommend you?" The missionary paused. "By the way, do you know what tithe is?"

"Yes, Pastor. After my father and I started worshiping in the Adventista chapel in Juanjuí, enemies came and carried off our belongings and burned our house down to the ground. For some reason, my father had kept his tithe in the house of a friend. It was quite a large amount—10 percent of the profits on animals we sold. Only the tithe escaped the fire and thievery."

Even this did not convince Pastor Pritchard. He said, "Look, the tithe is not a sign of discipleship. How can I know that you're truly converted?"

"Thank you, Pastor! I surely hope I can be baptized in the future." Leo tried to be polite, but inside the hurt felt like a knife cutting his heart. *The priest told me I'd never be worth anything. Anita's parents said I'm not good enough for their daughter. Now they don't want me in the Adventista Church. Well, they didn't say they don't want me, but I'm not good enough the way I am. Somebody's got to recommend me*, he agonized silently.

The youth congress ended with great disappointment for Leo, for he had not been baptized. Yet the "Share Your Faith" theme kept ringing in his ears. He found Julio López and presented him with a plan. "Why don't we make our trip back to Juanjuí a missionary trip? We can walk on the trails that follow the river and we can share our faith in all the villages along the way.

Leo continued as Julio stared with surprise. "I want to teach others to sing the beautiful choruses we learned here at the youth congress. I want to learn to preach."

Julio liked the idea. "You know, I have the same goals. Let's work together as a team."

Leo bought a new notebook so he could write down all the Bible texts they would use and also keep a record of their work. A Tarapoto church member heard of their plans and donated a Petromax kerosene lamp. Leo still had some of the money from Señora López, and he used it to buy spare mantles for the lantern.

On arrival at the first village, Juanguerra, the mayor gave the young men permission to hold a meeting in the school house. As soon as the first child entered the building, Leo began leading the singing of choruses while Julio played his guitar. Children, followed by parents, filled the building.

Long before the Bible study started, people who could not crowd into the classroom stood outside. These folks in this primitive area used only candles or sometimes a simple kerosene lamp with a wick. The novelty of the bright light of the Petromax mantle lantern proved a tremendous attraction.

The mayor became so enthusiastic over the success of the first meeting that he insisted that Leo and Julio stay a second night. They ended up spending three nights sharing the light of the Word and telling jungle families about Jesus, the Light of the world.

On the fourth day they started for Juanjuí. A few hours up the trail brought them to Buenos Aires, on the bank of the Huallaga River. There, city authorities offered the use of a chapel in the city hall. The young men lit their lantern and children began running in like butterflies to see the beautiful light. Fifty children arrived in just a few minutes. Then parents came and packed the building. They sang and prayed and preached for two nights before moving on to another village.

After 15 days they ran out of money. As they left San Rafael a man approached them. "My young brothers, you are working doing the work of God." He handed each of them a 10-sole bill, saying, "take this with you to help pay your expenses along the way." Leo had prayed for the windows of heaven to open. God blessed and both men thanked Him with full hearts.

It took a month for them to reach Leo's hometown of Juanjuí. They remembered how the disciples of Jesus returned from their missionary trips saying they lacked nothing. Leo recalled, "The Lord really did take care of us. We had a place to stay every night. We received fried eggs, boiled eggs, good bread, lots of fruit. And when we needed it most, we even received a gift of money. But the greatest gift has been the joy of seeing people hear about the soon coming of Jesus for their first time."

Something weighed on Leo's heart now that he was back home. He looked up Anita. "Please forgive me for breaking my appointment and going off to youth congress without even telling you," he said. "From here on, I can not be a part of your plans for life. I'm interested in spiritual things, and with Christ's help I'm determined to live a Christian life."

Anita seemed to understand and suggested, "Perhaps my parents were right after all." The two didn't see each other any more.

Two months passed. Leo received a letter from the Upper Amazon Mission headquarters, inviting him to attend another big meeting in Tarapoto—a colporteur rally. He didn't stop to think twice. He hastened to send a letter back to the mission advising he would attend.

Leo and Julio got together at the colporteur rally. On Friday night they were given opportunity to share experiences. Leo had kept careful notes of his missionary journey with Julio. He gave a complete report of what God did for them on the trip home from youth congress. There were many "amens."

After the meeting, Leo went to Pastor Pritchard. "When can I be baptized?" The mission president remembered their previous visit three months earlier. He looked at the young man and smiled. "I want to examine you."

He led Leo to a private room. With a Bible in one hand and the *Church Manual* in the other, he began asking questions. It frightened Leo at first and yet he found himself answering doctrinal questions with ease.

"You are doing very well, Leo. I can see that you have studied your Bible a great deal. Now I want to come to the most important question of all." The pastor looked directly at him. "Have you surrendered everything to Jesus? Have you confessed all your sins to Him? Have you made everything right with your fellow men?"

"Yes, Pastor! And I'm happy you didn't baptize me at the youth congress. When I got back to Juanjuí, I realized that I had broken a girl's heart. Anita and I planned to run away together. Every passion in my body made me want to go with her. But I knew it wasn't right. We would have been living in sin and even if we had decided to marry, she is not a Christian. I asked her to forgive me for going away without telling her. We haven't seen each other since. I know God has forgiven me."

Pastor Pritchard leaned forward. "You have confessed your sins and asked Jesus to let the Holy Spirit control your life. You may be baptized tomorrow afternoon at 3:00 o'clock."

"Oh, thank you, Pastor," Leo rejoiced. Because of his excitement, he hardly slept all night. He told himself, *At last I can become a member of God's true church. I can be part of the family of God.*

On Sabbath afternoon everyone walked to the river. Leo stood with other candidates. They sang, they prayed, they gave their testimony. Leo's turn came to walk into the river. The mission president raised his hand. "My dear brother Leo, because you love Jesus and have decided to leave the things of this world and follow Him, because you desire to be a son of God, I now baptize you in the name of the Father, and of the Son, and of the Holy Spirit."

The illegitimate son of the Amazon jungle—born again——Leo came up out of the water rejoicing to be a son of God. Words of scripture flashed in his memory: "He who overcomes shall inherit all things, and I will be his God and he shall be My Son" (Rev. 21:7).

The newly baptized members were introduced to each other. One was 18-year-old Maria, from San Roque. Leo looked at her dark wavy hair, soft brown eyes, and bashful smile. *She's the most beautiful girl I've ever seen,* he told himself. He soon learned that she was an orphan like him and lived with her grandmother.

Leo had become increasingly lonely since the death of his father. He had left a girl he thought he loved in order to follow Christ. Now he imagined *If I can just have a Christian girlfriend, someone to help me, someone to encourage me. Perhaps it's providential that Maria and I were baptized in the same baptism.*

Chapter 6

SWALLOWED BY A BOA

Behold, I give you the authority to trample on serpents and scorpions, and over all the power of the enemy, and nothing shall by any means hurt you. Luke 10:19.

A new dream began building in Leo's mind on the day of his baptism. He thought, *Even the Bible says, "It is not good that man should be alone." Maria could be the perfect answer to my prayers. She's a good girl. She lives up to the Bible requirements. It's evident that she loves to study God's Word.*

Even the church leaders recognized that a friendship between these two young people might be part of God's plan. One suggested, "Leo, if this friendship develops, the two of you could be colporteurs. You would make an excellent team."

Leo's baptism on September 23 turned into a happy day for many reasons. For years, he had felt torture when he recalled the circumstances of his birth. Now he felt the joy of a new birth—the thrill of being a son of God. With the enthusiasm of a newborn Christian he volunteered to become a literature evangelist. He dedicated his life to sharing the faith.

But as his mind turned to Maria, many questions arose. *Is it right for a young fellow like me, only 18 years old, to be thinking about getting married and starting a home? Is Maria really the one that God has planned for me? Will she remain faithful to Jesus and His church? Could we be happy together? Will she help me grow in my spiritual life?*

SWALLOWED BY A BOA

Leo knew he wanted her. He decided to wait and pray and make sure of what God wanted for him.

Leo's decision to colporteur resulted in a mission plan for him to work with Julio López, age 36, double the age of Leo. The two had worked successfully together for a month following youth congress.

They received instructions: "You men can walk to the Huallaga River and float down to Tierra Blanca on a balsa. From there you can take a river boat up the Ucayali to Pulcallpa. We'll ship books by airfreight and they will be waiting for you when you get there. Then you can build a balsa raft and float to Iquitos on the Amazon."

Leo hated to tell his new girlfriend good-bye, because he knew he would not see her again for many months. And since he would be traveling, with no schedule, he could not count on receiving letters.

Leo and Julio made record time in reaching Pucallpa where the books were waiting. In virgin forest just out of the city, they managed to cut 30 sturdy logs. They used these to construct a balsa raft large enough to carry 10 tons.

Few people on the Amazon have cash to pay for books, so they would have to trade them for all kinds of products. They needed lots of cargo space for cotton, raw rubber, yams, peanuts, chickens, turkeys, and sometimes even bows and arrows—anything that could later be sold for cash to pay the Book and Bible House.

In spite of their exciting mission for the Lord, both men felt lonely. While Leo wondered if he was too young to get married, Julio López kept thinking he might be getting too old. He knew an Adventista girl, Cecilia Navarro, in one of the first towns they visited, and decided to stay there. He told Leo, "You can go on down the river if you want. I'm staying around here until I get married."

Leo tried hard to sell books. But for three months he did not sell one book or magazine, and he planned to quit. One day he left his balsa tied up on the river bank and walked into a village called Nuevo Oriente. Here men were drilling for oil, and here he made his first sale. Now he thanked the Lord for giving him courage not to quit.

FUF-4

Leo began to have more success; in a few weeks he was joined by Julio and his new wife, who had caught a boat coming down river. Leo found it was great to have a cook, Cecilia, on board the balsa. He noticed how happy Julio was, and his own thoughts kept drifting back to Maria.

They followed the right bank of the river. Each day they stopped at little villages where they bartered books for produce. The large balsa served well as they took on more and more cargo. They built a chicken coop on board, which soon began to fill with chickens.

Navigating a balsa raft loaded with five tons of rice and other cargo became increasingly difficult. They steered with one oar, depending on the river current for propulsion. Because the raft was so hard to steer and the Ucayali was so wide, they always followed the right-hand shoreline.

One afternoon a heavy breeze came up; it kept blowing them to the left. The sky grew black, lightning flashed, winds increased, and waves began pouring over the log craft. Leo thought, *The only way to save our cargo is to get off the river and tie up on a nice sand bar until the storm is over.* They steered over to the edge of the river, but the bank was steep and their efforts to tie up failed. The heavy wind caught them again, pushing them toward the left shore.

The storm grew, pushing the raft back and forth on the river. Leo struggled with the steering oar to keep them from snagging on tree trunks that stuck out of the water. These could break the balsa raft into many pieces. "Hang on!" he shouted. Somehow as they crashed on the tree trunks, waves picked them up again and threw them against a muddy river bank. Leo leaped from the stern to avoid being washed overboard by the big waves.

Cecilia trembled as she looked at her colporteur husband. "I never bargained for a honeymoon like this," she said. The storm passed and they checked the damage. A few logs were broken and would need replacing, but basically the raft was intact. Leo breathed a prayer, "Thank you, God, for getting us off the dangerous tree trunks. We have a machete on board. I sharpened it yesterday and it's ready for work. I

SWALLOWED BY A BOA

know You'll help me find some good balsa trees." He hurried to shore, cut some fine logs, and brought them on board to make repairs.

He stood on the edge of the balsa raft, hacking at a new log to replace a broken one. Suddenly, the machete slipped from his hand and sank to the bottom of the dirty brown Ucayali. "Oh, no!" Leo cried. "All my hopes of making repairs just vanished with that machete. We have no other tools."

Leo called the newlyweds and they knelt with him on the log raft. "Thank you, Lord, for keeping us through the storm," they prayed. "Please help us find the machete."

Someone would have to dive into the river to find the lost machete. But down there danger lurked. During their weeks on the river they had seen men without arms, and others who were lame and limping. This was not because of car accidents, or because some train had run over them. It was because they had tangled with crocodiles.

When crocodiles are hungry they begin calling "um—um —um—um—um." The trio, Leo, Julio, and Cecilia, stood in silence. They heard the sound coming very clearly, "Um—um—um." The crocodiles in their river must be hungry. Besides that, the river was full of piranha—a small fish with razor-like teeth.

Leo and Julio exchanged glances. Julio, wanting to set a good example, volunteered to go down. He pulled off his clothes, except for a pair of shorts. "Pray for me," he said, and dove into the dark water. Leo and Cecilia waited. Finally Julio came up, but without the machete. He dove down twice, three times—still no machete. "I'm getting tired," he said. "The river must be 15 feet deep, and I can't find anything."

It was Leo who had lost the machete in the first place. "Let me take a turn," he said. He breathed deeply a few times, then he took another big breath and dove. He felt around in the mud on the bottom of the river. When he could hold his breath no longer he came back up. He dove in again and again. Five times. Fifteen times. Every now and then Leo felt piranha nibble his body and move away. He was almost exhausted when he dove the nineteenth time. He desperately needed to find the machete, but he came up without it.

He took another deep breath and dove in for the twentieth time. He kept praying and reaching around in the muddy river bottom. Just when he felt he would have to give up, his hand touched something hard. He gripped a piece of steel. "Thank You, God!" he almost shouted as he broke out above the water with the machete in his hand. The smiles on Julio's and Cecilia's faces were like those of treasure hunters who had just found gold.

Leo used the rescued machete to quickly repair the raft. With so many crocodiles and piranha around it didn't seem like a good place to spend the night, but it was really too late to search for a better place.

They ate a simple supper, had worship, and crawled into their mosquito nets. About an hour after dark, they heard a rustling among the chickens. Leo thought, *It might be a bat, or since one end of the raft is on the shore, some small animal may have come on board. One thing for sure—something is frightening the chickens.* He went out to check; finding nothing that could be causing the disturbance, he hurried back into his mosquito net.

Leo was almost asleep again when a big rooster on board let out a terrible scream. Leo hurried to one side of the raft while Julio went to the other side. Cecilia opened up the back part of her mosquito net, which was closest to the chickens, and screamed worse than the rooster. "It's a boa constrictor!" she shouted. "A big boa's got the rooster." The big snake was trying to swallow the rooster, but he couldn't seem to get past the rooster's wings.

Cecilia grabbed the rooster and tried to pull it free. Then all three people grabbed and pulled. The snake anchored its body around part of the raft. It showed more strength than two men and a woman plus the rooster struggling to free itself. The boa gave a big gulp and the rooster disappeared. The snake slipped away in the darkness.

More happened than they realized. Leo said, "I think we'd better count our chickens." Fifteen chickens and the rooster were missing! "Now what are we going to do?" he murmured. "How will we ever pay for our books and get our accounts settled with the Book and Bible House? The treasurer won't give us credit for chickens swallowed by a boa."

They discussed the problem and decided to get some sleep. They reckoned, "If the boa has eaten 15 chickens and a rooster, it should have a full stomach and not bother us anymore."

They weren't in their mosquito nets for two minutes when the chickens began moving from one side to the other in the coop. The trio raced back out. In the dark shadows they could see the entire length of the giant snake reaching more than 30 feet up onto the shore; its head was in the chicken coop.

Julio López raised the machete high over his head. With all the strength he could muster—and he was more than six feet tall—he brought the knife down onto the snake. The machete glanced off the snake as though the snake were a piece of steel; the blade made only a small cut in the snake's neck.

They watched the boa disappear into the river. It swished around as though it might be suffering. The bleeding from the nick in its neck would attract piranha. These small fish with razorlike teeth waste no time devouring their victims. Leo suggested, "It's time for another prayer meeting. A boa that's still hungry after eating 15 chickens and a rooster could have eaten any one of us. It would have no problem eating a man more than six feet tall."

They knelt together under the Amazon stars and thanked God for His protection that afternoon and evening. He had helped them through the tempest and wind. He kept the raft from being broken to pieces by the tree trunks. He had protected them from piranhas and crocodiles. He had saved them from the boa. Surely, "The angel of the Lord encamps all around those who fear Him, and delivers them" (Ps. 34:7). They never saw the boa again.

Leo watched Julio's and Cecilia's joy and happiness increase with each new day. To Julio, he referred to his reaction as "holy envy," but he didn't admit that thoughts of romance filled his own heart. He kept dreaming about Maria, the beautiful girl he met on the day of his baptism.

He believed that if God intended for him to marry Maria, there would surely be some providential guidance. He began fasting every Sabbath, asking the Lord to reveal His will.

One night Leo woke up. *What have I been dreaming?* he asked himself. *I just saw Maria in a dance hall; she had a cigarette in her mouth.* When morning came he realized he'd had the same dream three times during the night. He questioned, *Is the Lord trying to tell me something?*

After six months the colporteurs reached the river port of Iquitos, headquarters for the Upper Amazon Mission. They worked hard to sell all the produce they had amassed, in order to make a cash settlement with the Book and Bible House. God blessed, and the gain more than made up for the loss of chickens swallowed by a boa.

Leo remembered how God had protected when he dove into water filled with crocodiles and piranhas, and how he had been spared from the belly of a boa. He prayed, "Lord, you know my need. Please save me from my loneliness. You know how I feel about Maria. But Lord, may Your will be done!"

Chapter 7

DREADING THE DRAFT

Therefore gird up the loins of your mind, be sober, and rest your hope fully upon the grace that is to be brought to you at the revelation of Jesus Christ; as obedient children, not conforming yourselves to the former lusts, as in your ignorance; but as He who called you is holy, you also be holy in all your conduct . . . . Having been born again, not of corruptible seed but incorruptible, through the word of God which lives and abides forever" 1 Peter 1:13, 14, 15, 23.

Leo's lonely heart longed for the girl from San Roque. He had spent six long months in remote jungle, with no way of communicating with her. After settling accounts for his books, he inquired about Maria. He learned she had left the church; on the very night he dreamed of seeing her in a dance hall, she had married a young policeman in her home town. He thought, *God's answer is clear. I must accept His will.*

Now Julio wanted to settle down with his new wife, so the mission asked Leo to return to Pucallpa alone. He built another balsa raft, took a load of books, and headed out for six more months of adventure, this time on the left shore of the Ucayali.

While Leo sold books, a new idea filled his mind. *I would like to become a pastor. I want to do more to help people get ready for the coming of Jesus. But what hope is there? I don't even have a high school education. I've never attended a church with a pastor, where I could watch and learn from someone with lots of experience in the Lord's work.*

Soon after reaching Iquitos again, Leo celebrated his nineteenth birthday. Peruvian law required that all males reaching 19 register for army service. He registered, and it caused him a new concern.

The Peruvian military followed the practice of casting lots to see who would actually be called into the army. Leo worried, *What if my number comes up? Will I have to leave my work as a literature evangelist and rush away to some army barracks? Will I be able to follow the dictates of my conscience? What could army life be like? Will I be persecuted for my faith?*

Leo knew of youth who had been faithful during their early years in the church but when they went into the army they lost their faith.

Some church members in Iquitos, impressed with Leo's spirituality, asked, "Have you been in the army yet?"

"No, I haven't."

"That's too bad. We see you enthusiastic for the things of Christ. When you come back from military service, you will have forgotten all about religion. They all come back smoking, drinking, swearing, fighting and looking for women."

Leo agreed that any Adventista who returned from military service like that certainly failed to honor Jesus and His church. All this caused him to think even more seriously about his own relationship with his Saviour and his need for staying very close to God through Bible study and prayer.

He mused, *Being a true Christian is surely more than living right when circumstances are favorable. It's not difficult to be an Adventista when you have Sabbaths free and there is no persecution. But what will it be like when these privileges are taken away?*

He asked God to keep him true. *I must be ready to honor Jesus and not work even one hour on the Sabbath. I must guard the edges of the Sabbath. It will not be proper for me to study army material on Friday night or take an examination on Sabbath. There will be many tests. Satan will try to break me down. It will take a miracle for me to stand faithful always.*

Leo recalled the miracles that already had taken place in his life. *My mother placed me in the hands of a witch doctor*

DREADING THE DRAFT

because I was dying. I know God healed me. When I turned 6, wicked politicians ordered my father killed, but the Lord spared him, along with my sister and me.

At 12, I was tempted by billiards and smoking to a life of vice. God came into my life through the priest's Bible, and saved me from disaster. At 18, I planned to run away with a girl friend to live a life of fornication and lust. God saved me from this by using a minister's wife to invite me to attend a youth congress. While selling books and Bibles, I could have ended up inside the stomach of a boa, but God sent His angel to protect me.

The possibility of being called into the army remained a major source of anxiety. Leo prayed fervently, "Lord, give me mercy. I don't have a father to counsel me. I have no mother by my side, or even a sister or brother. I'm just an orphan boy from the jungle. Help me to know how to be faithful if I get drafted into the military."

The Amazon Mission sent a new literature evangelist to work with Leo. His new partner, Manuel Gonzales, unlike Julio, continually tormented him. "Leo, you think you're more of a saint than anyone else. I can assure you that you are not. What do you think you are doing, fasting away the Sabbath? Do you think it makes you a better Christian?"

Leo looked at Manuel without saying a word. He reasoned, *There's no way Manuel can understand the conflict that's going on inside of me.*

As Leo was selling books in Pucallpa, he received a certified letter. It read:

"Señor Leonardo Pinedo:

"Please report to military headquarters in Iquitos immediately. You are being inducted into the Peruvian army."

His first reaction was disappointment. *Why, God, did you let this happen?* He knew the Lord had blessed his literature ministry with sales of thousands of soles worth of Adventista publications. He loved working for God. Would it be possible to work for God and country? He quoted the words of Jesus, "Render therefore to Caesar the things that are Caesar's, and to God the things that are God's" (Matt. 12:21).

He determined to accept what he could not change. *I can't pass up the opportunity to be a good citizen,* he thought. He checked at the port, but there were no riverboats going to Iquitos. There were no airlines flying that route at the time. There was no practical way to get to Iquitos.

The captain in charge of army inductions for Pucallpa learned about Leo's predicament, for Leo had sold him several books. He said, "Look, young man, there are daily flights to Lima. Why don't you enter the army there? My office can work out a transfer for you." Leo agreed, and this officer took care of the necessary documentation changes. Within a few days Leo held the transfer documentation in his hand.

In late December he flew to Lima, capital of Peru. The small DC-3 airliner in which he flew climbed to over 18,000 feet in order to clear the peaks of the Andes. The stewardess brought oxygen to all the passengers. The tiny aircraft bounced around a great deal and Leo tried to help his air-sick seatmate.

Once on the ground in Lima, Leo made it his first business to look for leaders of the Adventistas. He found a missionary, Pastor Richard Hayden, who treated him kindly and put him in touch with Pastor Francisco Scarcella, evangelist for the Inca Union Mission.

Leo confided to the latter, "Pastor, I've been drafted. But before checking into the barracks, I want to counsel with you. I'm determined to be faithful regardless of what happens to me."

Pastor Scarcella reassured him, "Don't worry! I have a friend, Commander Salinas, who will help us. Get into my car. Let's go see him now."

Away they drove, through heavy Lima traffic. Everyone seemed to be in a rush. Horns honked, brakes squealed—so very different from the slow pace of the Amazon jungle. The pastor saw Leo brace himself several times. "You'll get used to this. All the people here in the city drive like they are crazy," he smiled.

DREADING THE DRAFT

Commander Salinas greeted his old friend, Pastor Scarcella. "By the way," he said, "I'll be happy to do whatever I can to help you."

Francisco Scarcella introduced Leo and explained, "This young man wants to continue serving the Lord even after he gets in the army. Is there any way you can help him get Sabbaths off so he can attend church?"

The kind commander assured him that this would be no problem. He turned to Leo. "Just wait and present yourself at the barracks on the first of February," he said. "Once you get checked in, ask for me. I will put you in a place where no one will bother you regarding your religious convictions."

As Leo and the pastor drove away, the younger man was too happy to pay any attention to the mad traffic. "Pastor Scarcella," he said, "God is answering my prayers. He is putting His hand over me. I can't thank Him enough. Commander Salinas accepted your suggestion to arrange for me to keep the Sabbath and attend church."

Pastor Scarcella helped Leo find a place to stay near the Inca Union Mission Headquarters while he waited for induction. During this time Leo made many new Adventista friends. One of these learned that Leo was entering the army. "Don't be foolish," this friend said. "Why are you going into the army? Two years of your life will be lost —wasted. We can get you out of going into the army. I have a friend who has done favors like this for many young men, including my own sons. He knows how to keep people out of the army."

"How can this be done?" Leo asked with amazement.

"Well, he charges only 300 soles and then he takes care of everything."

"But what does he do?" Leo wanted to know.

"My friend is a lawyer; he knows what to do. He makes all the arrangements. He has army friends and everything is taken care of, provided he gets his money. It's a terrific deal—you just pay 300 soles and get out of serving in the army. It might be a little difficult to get a hold of that much money, but you can raise it. Believe me, it's worth it to get out of two years in the army."

Leo thought, *What a great idea. I could return to colporteuring or perhaps go to school.* On the last day of January he went to see Pastor Scarcella. The pastor greeted him. "How is everything going?" he asked. "Are you ready for life in the barracks?"

"Well, Pastor, more or less . . ."

"What do you mean, 'more or less'? We've already made arrangements with the commander and you've got to go."

"Well, Pastor . . . uh, well, you see, I guess there's a way of getting out of the army. It really isn't necessary to go."

"What do you mean by this, Leo?"

"I just discovered that I can pay a lawyer 300 soles and he'll fix up my papers. I won't have to serve in the army at all. There won't be any worry about having to work on Sabbath. No one will try to force me to drink. No one will corrupt my life by getting me to dance or go to shows. I've thought a lot about this, Pastor. The thing for me to do is to avoid the army."

"Leo, tell me—are you ready to go into the army and be faithful to your God?"

"I don't know, Pastor."

"Haven't you prayed and fasted and asked God to help you? Aren't you going to give God a chance to answer your prayers?"

"Pastor, I guess I haven't completely made up my mind."

Pastor Scarcella asked, "Do you want me to tell you the truth?"

Leo replied, "Go ahead, Pastor. I'm ready to listen."

"Look, this lawyer will have to falsify your documents in order for you not to serve. In reality, there is no reason why you shouldn't go. You are among those on whom the lot has fallen.

"If you are willing now to break the laws of the country to get out of going into the army, tomorrow you will have no scruples against breaking the law of God. What do you say? Are you going into the army or are you going to try and find some dishonest way to stay out?" The evangelist searched Leo's face.

DREADING THE DRAFT

"But Pastor, I don't want to be in the army. Besides, other 'Adventistas' have paid and they stayed out."

"You'll have to decide, Leo. Are you going to follow some weak church member or are you going to stand strong for Christ as an honest and true son of God?"

"That's enough, Pastor. I'm going to the army. Tomorrow is the first of February. Please take me right now."

Pastor Scarcella opened the door of his car and Leo go it. They drove directly to the barracks at the San Bartolome Army Induction Center, where Leo got out. Leo thanked the pastor for the advice and for the trip, then he watched the man drive away and disappear into the traffic. *I wished he could have stayed with me until I'm sworn into the army*, he mused.

Leo signed in at the main office. He presented his induction letter. "Now, where's your birth certificate?" asked the inducting officer. "Oh, you're an illegitimate. You'd better be careful how you handle yourself around here!"

Leo completed filling out forms, made a pledge of loyalty to his country, and took an aptitude test. He was officially a soldier in the Peruvian army now. He remembered the promise of help from Pastor Scarcella's friend and made a request, "I'd like to see Commander Salinas."

The induction officer replied, "Sorry! Commander Salinas has just been transferred to a new assignment far from Lima." A shock wave passed over Leo. He could not say a word.

Chapter 8

SABBATH IN UNIFORM

You therefore must endure hardship as a good soldier of Jesus Christ. 2 Timothy 2:4.

Angry thoughts flashed through Leo's mind. *Why did Pastor Scarcella get me into this mess? He didn't even stay to make sure that everything would work out. How will I ever keep the Sabbath now? Why didn't I just pay the lawyer?*

Within minutes, Leo found himself boarding a big truck. The commander shouted, "How many boys do we have here?"

"Eighty," came the reply.

"I need 20 more," the commander yelled. Twenty additional men were herded in like cattle. One hundred new recruits squeezed into the open truck.

Thinking of his own fate, Leo forgot about all the men squeezed around him. Silently he prayed, "Lord, help me to be faithful. Make me willing to endure hardship as a good soldier of Jesus."

After receiving his uniforms, Leo asked for an interview with his captain. Providence smiled and the interview was granted. Leo, still in civilian clothes, sat in front of Captain Hugo Sotillo. For hours he explained his Christian way of life and his determination to remain faithful to Jesus and His church.

"Captain, I want to be a good soldier, I want to cooperate, I want to work, I want to study and do my best. First of all though, I must honor Jesus."

After listening rather patiently, Captain Sotillo said sarcastically to Leo, "Don't worry, young man. I've been an officer for more than 20 years. During the first days of service there are always a few new recruits who come and talk with me. They say, 'Listen, Captain, I'm Protestant,' or 'I'm Baptist,' or 'I'm Adventist'—'My parents are Jews.'

"I want you to know that every time, in less than eight days they are drinking, dancing, gambling. They do everything that everyone else does in the military service. So don't worry, son! In a few days we'll be drinking beer together. We'll have a lot of fun dancing with the girls that visit our army base.

"Just forget all about your civilian life! When you leave my office, you will take off your civilian clothes and put on your army uniform. With that uniform, all the responsibilities of the past will be forgotten.

"I want you to understand that you will do what we ask you to do. You will eat what we ask you to eat. You'll work any day we ask you to work. And if you don't—you'll do it by force, even if we have to kick you. Don't bother me with any more childish things from civilian life."

With hope fading from his heart, Leo thought, *I'd better make use of this last opportunity while I'm without a uniform.* He stood and faced the officer across a large desk. "Captain," he said, "I didn't come here to joke or speak lightly. I've shared what's on my heart. I want you to know right now that if I have trouble during my military service, it will be because of my religious convictions. My conscience does not allow me to change my convictions for anything in the world—not even to obey you.

"My first priority will be to please God. Captain, I understand what you said. I want you to know that I've presented the true reasons for my faith and conduct. If you're not able to help me, I'm ready to suffer the consequences."

Captain Sotillo moved toward Leo. "Leave me now. I don't want to talk with you about this anymore! Do you understand?"

Leo went to his barracks, removed his civilian clothes, and put on his uniform. He thought, *On the day of my baptism, Pastor Pritchard read, "For as many of you as were baptized into Christ have put on Christ." They can make me take off civilian clothes, but they will never make me take off Christ."*

Late Monday afternoon the men in Leo's group were called together for orientation. They learned about the different bugle calls—which was the signal to wake up, which was the signal to go to sleep, which for meals, and many others. Orientation continued for the rest of the week. Leo learned how to march, how to care for his clothes and barracks, and all the details of army life.

All this time Leo wondered, *How will I spend my first Sabbath in the army? The friendly commander has moved away. The captain intends to destroy all my religious convictions. What can I do?*

Friday morning Leo went back to the captain. Saluting the officer, he said, "Captain, tomorrow is Sabbath. I want you to know that beginning with sunset tonight, I will not be able to take further part in the activities of the soldiers."

Captain's Sotillos's eyes narrowed in anger. "And what do you want from me?" he demanded.

"Captain, my conscience compels me to keep the Bible Sabbath! I must remember the Sabbath and keep it holy."

The captain growled, "Get out of here and don't see me again!"

From the barracks window, Leo watched the sun set, indicating that his first Sabbath in the army had begun. Each time the bugle sounded, he remained in his barracks. He knew very well what the different calls meant. Even when they called the troops to eat, he stayed. He decided it would be his custom to fast and pray during the hours of the Sabbath. He felt a special need for help from the Lord.

Lieutenant Manual A. Odria headed Leo's section. On Sabbath morning he noticed that one new recruit failed to

SABBATH IN UNIFORM 65

participate in the activities. He walked over to Leo. "Look, something is happening to you, young fellow. What's the matter?"

"Sir, today is the holy Sabbath. I notice our schedule calls for us to clean up camp and report for inspection. I want you to know that I can not take part."

"What's the trouble, soldier? Are you sick?" the lieutenant snapped.

"No, sir, I feel very well." Leo spoke directly to the officer: "Sir, I'm an Adventista—a Seventh-day Adventist. My conscience does not permit me to do any kind of secular work on Sabbath."

The lieutenant's face changed. His reply was not what Leo expected to hear: "Don't worry, son. I've served in Puno at 12,500 feet elevation in the Andes. It's one of the most difficult places in Peru. You've got to be rugged to make it up there. Puno is headquarters for the Lake Titicaca Mission. I know a great deal about the work of Adventistas. I learned to appreciate the work of Adventist missionaries who came to our country from overseas.

"Peru owes a great debt to the Adventist work. Millions of Aymara and Quechua Indians lived for centuries in ignorance. They were slaves to coca and alcohol. Missionaries came and established schools and churches. They have transformed thousands of these people and brought them back to civilization.

"I want you to know that I'm here to help you. I will be your protector in the army." Odria reached into his pocket and withdrew something. "Please take these keys to my apartment," he said.

Leo could not believe his ears. As he accepted the keys, Lieutenant Odria continued, "Go to my apartment—take your Bible—close the door. No one will bother you. If anyone makes a fuss, I'm responsible. My uncle is president of Peru. You can count on me to help you."

Leo marveled how God's hand worked in a way he never dreamed possible. "With God's help I can keep the Sabbath in uniform." He ran to the barracks and picked up his Bible and Sabbath school quarterly. The bugle sounded—time for soldiers to go out and work. But not for him. He could take time to worship his Creator. With Bible in hand, he went to Lieutenant Odria's apartment and closed the door. He knew he wasn't alone. Jesus was there with him.

In the meantime, the captain missed Leo and asked, "Where is Pinedo? What's with this young soldier? Has he deserted?"

Lieutenant Odria answered simply, "He's in my apartment doing what I asked him to do." But the lieutenant realized someone had to do Leo's work. So he himself did the cleanup work that Leo was supposed to do. He wanted to be sure that his unit passed inspection.

No one was required to work on Sabbath afternoon. At lunchtime the lieutenant checked on Leo. "Son," he said, "I've done the best I could for you. The captain is difficult. He wanted you to come and do your work. He said you would never learn unless you did it. I told him I would do it and not to be concerned. Our unit passed inspection.

"It worked out all right today, but to avoid future problems we must make a better plan. Every officer is allowed to assign a soldier to be his special helper. How would you like to be my helper?"

"Sure, Lieutenant. It's my desire to cooperate as long as there is a way to be at peace with my conscience and in harmony with God," Leo replied with gratitude. The new assignment, however, led to a new problem.

A few days later the captain called the officers of his company and asked them to bring their personal helpers to his office. The helpers were really personal servants. They shined shoes, made beds, swept, cleaned boots, groomed horses. They made sure the officer had clean clothes and clean towels, and they ran errands. One who accepted these assignments became ineligible for army promotions.

Officers were asked to choose men of inferior ability for their personal service. Lieutenant Odria risked violating army procedures by choosing Leo. Captain Sotillo protested his choice, saying, "I need this man and he shouldn't be a helper for anyone."

SABBATH IN UNIFORM

Lieutenant Odria snapped back, "I need a helper who is alert and intelligent. That's why I chose him."

Later he confided to Leo, "I'm running a risk in trying to help you keep your Sabbath, but I hope to get away with it because my name is Odria."

Soldiers were obliged to wash their clothing every Sabbath in order to be ready for Special Inspection on Sunday. Each recruit had only two uniforms. One was worn all week. Orders were to wash the uniform on Sabbath. Anyone who did not comply would spend a day in jail and have all privileges suspended.

Leo always waited until after sundown on Sabbath to wash his uniform. Then he hung it near the chimney that came through from the kitchen. By midnight it was dry. He ironed it and stood ready for inspection early Sunday morning.

Even officers' personal helpers were required to perform some duties on Sabbath. Lieutenant Odria got into trouble with the captain because he had others to do what Leo was supposed to do.

One morning Odria called Leo. "It's not working out for you to be my personal helper," he said. "We need a better way to help you keep your Sabbaths. Go to my apartment and wrap up a few shirts. Go to the main gate of the barracks and tell the guard you are going to my house with orders from me. Don't tell him anything else. After you stop at my house and leave the shirts with my wife, go worship God in the manner your Bible says. God bless you! I'll be responsible for your absence."

Leo stopped first at the officer's home and then went directly to the Miraflores Seventh-day Adventist church in Lima. He had been in the army for three months and this was his first chance to come back and meet with the Adventistas.

Sabbath school had just begun. The only empty seats were near the front. Leo walked forward as heads turned and eyes stared at a soldier in uniform. The superintendent paused a few seconds, surprised to see someone from the military, and then he gave him a welcome.

Leo enjoyed the Sabbath school and worship services more than ever before. When the services ended, members surrounded him, along with Pastor Scarcella and Dr. Clayton Potts, missionary director of the Good Hope Clinic.

Leo joined the brethren for a fellowship dinner. Pastor Scarcella delighted to learn how Leo had stood faithful to his principles for Sabbath observance.

At the Adventist youth meeting that afternoon, Leo shared some of his experiences as a literature evangelist in the Amazon. He requested that all pray that God would keep him true during his army service. After sundown, he returned to the army base.

Almost at once, his absence created a tense situation. Early Monday morning Leo received a call to the captain's office. He asked with a growl, "Were you gone on Saturday? Where did you go?"

Leo determined to tell the truth. "Yes, Captain, I was gone all day Sabbath and I'll tell you where I went."

The scowling captain burst back, "You went to church didn't you?"

"Yes, Captain, I went to the Miraflores Adventista church."

"You know very well, Pinedo, the army has rules and you'd better watch out. You could pay dearly for the things that you and Lieutenant Odria have been doing. How would you like to be sent up for court-martial?"

Chapter 9

HIGH JUMP

From evening to evening, you shall celebrate your sabbath." Lev. 23:32.

The captain's threat of a military trial and the possible consequences worried Leo, but he decided to keep his mouth shut. He didn't want to make matters worse by saying the wrong thing. Lieutenant Odria had stuck his neck out for Leo time after time. Although Leo had escaped thus far, he thought, *What will happen to me if Lieutenant Odria ever gets transferred? I must keep trusting the Lord and leave my life in His hands.* He praised God that three months of basic training were over, and with God's help he had been able to keep every Sabbath.

Leo attended his army classes and studied energetically. He took careful notes and always responded with the right answer when questions were asked. Although the captain hated the young soldier's Sabbath, he felt a certain sympathy for a young man who learned so quickly. Many times he loaned Leo his books of army rules asking him to review his notes and teach his classes. The captain would make use of the time to break away and visit friends or take a walk.

One evening the bugle sounded and Captain Sotillo called his company together. "Men, we have a very important announcement. We have been watching the activities of the men who just completed basic training. Private Leo Pinedo, please come forward!"

Leo's heart thumped. *The captain has figured out a way to humiliate me in front of all the men because of my Sabbath.* He marched to the front, faced the captain, and saluted.

The captain turned to the men in his company and announced, "Men, in this special ceremony, we are promoting Private Leo Pinedo to sergeant." Turning to Leo he said, "Congratulations, Sergeant Pinedo!"

Leo gasped. *Could this be true? Are my ears confusing signals?* It was true, and a wave of relief swept over him.

His promotion meant more responsibility and more work for Leo. It would also mean a little higher rate of salary, although at best his pay would remain a miserable amount compared to what he could earn in civilian life.

Sergeant Leo Pinedo was now the leader of 14 men, with whom he was to be at all times. A new question troubled him. *Now what am I going to do about the Sabbath?* he wondered. *Does the captain, after all, have some ulterior motive for getting me into this?*

Lieutenant Odria came to his rescue. "Look, Sergeant," he said. "Don't be too concerned. I'll be in charge of the men on Sabbath. You do everything you can during the week, and on Sabbath I'll take over your men. You can spend Sabbath in my apartment."

Leo thought, *This is working well, but I must always remember that Sabbath is a day of 24 hours. It's not just Sabbath morning and Sabbath afternoon. I must continue honoring the Sabbath from Friday sunset to Saturday sunset.*

Even officers such as Lieutenant Odria who showed sympathy for Leo and his religious convictions had a hard time understanding why he needed a full 24 hours.

One Friday morning the captain called his company together. "Men, our battalion commander is sponsoring track and field events. All six companies will compete against each other. You've been practicing since you were inducted. Now you must practice to win. Our company must win! The track and field competition will take place in eight days."

He turned to Leo. "And you, Sergeant Pinedo. Don't think that these events are only for privates. You have a strong body. You've been jumping over logs, paddling canoes, and walking and running in the Amazon jungle. With your strong legs, I'm expecting you to qualify for the 100-meter race, the broad jump, and the high jump. You had better spend every minute practicing so you can be ready for the events next Friday."

"Yes, Captain," Leo responded. "I'll do my best." He approached the captain to say something privately. "Please remember that I won't be doing any practice for athletic events from sundown tonight until after sundown tomorrow night. I believe that after resting on God's holy Sabbath, He will give me strength to do better on the other days of the week."

The Captain eyed Leo in disgust. "All you think about is this Sabbath! You better start thinking about winning!"

Early the next Friday morning Leo knelt by the bed in his barracks and prayed, "Dear Father, you have been so good to me. Thank you for not allowing these athletic events to be held on Sabbath. You heard the captain say that no one could miss these events under any circumstances. Please help me do my best. Touch the captain's heart so he will have consideration for my religious convictions."

The battalion's six companies of 1,000 men each assembled for the track and field events. Each of the six captains was determined that his company would present the winning team. Men shouted and screamed when their team participated. Leo came in first in the 100-meter race. His broad jump covered the greatest distance of any contestant. His company led with the highest scores. Could they hold this position?

Tension mounted as the final event, the high jump, came up. Fortunately the men got a brief rest before jumping. Within minutes it all narrowed down to just two men—Private Saúl Sánchez and Sergeant Leo Pinedo. On the next try, Saúl Sánchez tripped the crossbar. They gave him two more tries and each time he failed.

Leo prayed silently: "Lord, You know I'm tired. These men make fun of my Sabbath and ridicule me for refusing pork and eating lots of fruits and vegetables. Please Lord, give me special strength."

He faced the crossbar from a 45-degree angle and began a slow, controlled run. In the last few steps he picked up speed. From a crouched position in front of the bar, he sprang high. He felt like the hand of an angel took hold of his body and lifted him higher. He flew over the bar, and the crowd of soldiers applauded.

The bar was raised two centimeters. Leo went over again. They raised it another three centimeters. Leo went right over. They put it up five more centimeters; it now measured at two meters high. Leo cleared the bar. The soldiers roared and screamed. Not exactly a world record, but six and a half feet is an excellent jump for a short Peruvian.

Leo's captain ran up shouting, "We've won! We've won!" He gave Leo a big *abrazo* and then invited him to join him and other officers for a special dinner.

In the afternoon, the captain called Leo to his office. "Your top physical condition, Leo, put our company ahead of every other in our battalion. Because of this I am going to give you an entire week free. During this time you can do anything you want."

The captain handed Leo seven passes, all signed. He had put down the dates of seven consecutive Sundays. It was late Friday afternoon and Leo knew his Sabbath would begin in just an hour. He smiled at his captain.

"Sir, instead of giving me Sunday, why don't you give me Sabbaths free?" he asked.

"Well, since I made you the promise of a week off to do anything you want, I guess we'll have to do it that way," the captain agreed. He signed seven new passes for seven consecutive Sabbaths and handed them to Leo.

Leo felt like jumping and shouting—almost two months of Sabbaths free without the need to bother any military officer with his special requests. And the captain had marked his passes from sundown Friday to sundown Saturday.

"Thank you, Captain, for all your kindness to me today," Leo said.

The officer nodded. "It does seem that you have taken full advantage of your opportunity. I did promise, so you may go now."

Leo really cared little about winning the athletic contests, but he rejoiced to see how the Lord used this to move the heart of the captain to give him Sabbaths free. He didn't know that although the captain was extremely happy for the success of his team, it would not be long until he would totally repent of ever signing the seven Sabbath passes.

Other soldiers watched with envy when Leo took his Sabbath leaves. They began calling him a fanatical Protestant. In spite of these accusations, seeds of truth were planted in the hearts of many soldiers. Leo's faith sharing led 85 men to enroll in the Spanish Voice of Prophecy radio Bible course. Four men secretly studied the Sabbath school lesson every day with Leo. Many others came and asked him questions about the Bible.

The captain heard that Leo was carrying out what he called "religious proselytizing." He called for him. "Look, Pinedo, this is where you've made your big mistake. Don't you know that in this place, nothing is to be taught except the Catholic religion?

"If you have religious convictions, OK. Keep them in your own head and heart. Please don't try to put these ideas into the minds of other soldiers. You are not permitted to do this. It is totally against the rules of the Peruvian armed forces. The Roman Catholic Church is the official church of the state. The armed forces have the responsibility of teaching only this religion. We have a chaplain here to give spiritual instruction. We don't want any Protestant propaganda."

This distressed Leo. *What can I do with all the men who are studying the Voice of Prophecy Bible Courses?* he asked himself. *The interested men are equal to half a company or eight and a half percent of our battalion. They keep coming to me with their Bible questions.*

The captain found Leo reading the Bible with Private Ramirez (who later received baptism, graduated from Inca

Union College, and entered the teaching ministry). The captain accused Leo of flagrant violation of the internal rules of the army and specific orders he had given. He said, "I don't want to see you with this book any more. If you've got to read the Bible, go read it to yourself. But don't ever show this book to your fellow soldiers."

A new turn of events brought discouragement to Leo. Since Leo's first day in the service, Lieutenant Odria had encouraged him to follow his religious convictions. Now this officer was transferred to Caracas. With Odria absent, the captain renewed his efforts to break Leo. No longer could he attend church on Sabbath. He spent Sabbaths in the barracks, where he read his Bible.

The captain couldn't get Sergeant Pinedo out of the barracks, so he went there and began teaching a class. Leo decided not to listen on Sabbath. The captain called him to the blackboard. Leo stood up, but refused to talk. The Captain swore. "You stupid idiot! You illegitimate, filthy bastard!"

Leo remembered hearing words like that when he was only a boy playing in the streets of Contamana. He thought to himself, *I only wish that this poor captain could learn the joy of being born again. I'm thrilled that the Bible teaches I'm a brother of Jesus as long as I do His Father's will. They called Jesus a lot worse things than they've ever called me.*

Lieutenant Odria returned, and Leo told him about his problem. The young officer went to see Commander Flores. The commander smiled. "This captain is a difficult man," he said. "But don't worry about Pinedo while he is under my care."

The commander called for Sergeant Leo Pinedo on Friday morning. "I understand you haven't been able to attend religious services for some time," he said.

"Yes, Commander, that's true. The captain has not given me permission to go and worship for quite a while."

"Sit down," said the commander. "I've got a solution. My friend, missionary Richard Hayden, loaned me a book, *The Great Controversy*. I've finished the book and want to return it to him. You can go to your worship service tomorrow morning and give it to him. Take this pass to your captain. I've written a note asking him to sign it for you."

Joy filled Leo's heart. "Thank you very much, Commander." He took the book, saluted, and started out to find Captain Sotillo. He found him in his office. Leo faced him. "I hate to bother you, Captain, but I have a pass that needs your signature."

"What pass is this? Don't you know I'm the only one that gives orders around here?" he barked.

Leo eyed the captain. "Do you mean to say that I'm not under orders from the commander of this battalion?"

The captain acted uncomfortable and said simply, "No one is to leave. Even if the commander gave this order, there is no reason for you to leave."

"But Captain, I have a book here in my hand. The commander ordered me to take this book to its owner."

"What book?"

"It's a book that he borrowed from a friend and wants returned."

"It seems you are able to find any pretext in order to leave," the captain snarled. After talking with the secretary, he signed Leo's pass. He stood up, handed Leo the pass —and slapped him in the face. "Get out of here! I never want to see you again."

After an absence of many weeks, Leo walked into the Miraflores Adventista church once again, this time carrying a copy of *The Great Controversy* for Pastor Hayden. Each week the commander arranged a way for Leo to get a pass, and every Sabbath church members awaited his arrival with anticipation. He always told them about some new blessing the Lord had given him.

Not only did Leo go to the morning worship services, but some 20 to 30 soldiers began joining him in attending the youth meetings on Sabbath afternoons. Nothing like this had ever happened in the history of the Miraflores church. It began to look like a military chapel.

The soldiers who attended the Sabbath afternoon youth meetings were servicemen whom Leo had enrolled in the Voice of Prophecy Bible correspondence course. They were studying the Bible, learning about the Sabbath, and even studying the Sabbath school lesson quarterly. They read their Morning Watch and tried to fulfill their duties to God.

Church members delighted to see what was happening. Their city church had never experienced anything like this before.

Leo's good fortune soon faded. His special friends at the army base left. Lieutenant Odria transferred to another battalion. Commander Flores joined a special diplomatic delegation to another South American country.

The new battalion commander, Cardeña Caro, from Cusco, learned that certain privileges with passes had been granted on Sabbath. He announced, "Effective immediately, no one will be granted Sabbath leaves."

Leo's captain smiled. "At last we have a commander who is going to back me up," he said.

Leo went to have a talk with the new commander. He stood in the military forum at the side of the commander, who asked, "Sergeant, what is your request?"

Offering a silent prayer, Leo spoke in a firm voice. "Sir, in Peru we have freedom of worship. "I'm a Seventh-day Adventist. The previous commander gave me permission to attend church on my Sabbath."

Commander Caro broke in. "Don't say another word about that. Do you think the army is like the house of your grandmother? It's precisely these privileges that we're going to stop. From now on, no one will have a Sabbath pass for any reason!"

Chapter 10

FLAGS AT HALF MAST

Be faithful unto death, and I will give you the crown of life. Rev. 2:10.

"No Sabbath passes for any reason!" Leo listened as Commander Cardeña Caro challenged him. "You are to understand that in the military, your spiritual life is dictated by the Catholic religion. Everyone inducted into the army is obligated to practice the rites and ceremonies of the church. Sergeant Pinedo, I have nothing more to say. Get out of here now, and get out fast!"

Leo walked away, realizing that a church-army plot had already been made against him. The captain had informed the commander that Sergeant Leo Pinedo did not attend Mass. Also, he did not attend religious instruction, where he would be obliged to kneel and make the sign of the cross contrary to his conscience.

The chaplain held the rank of captain. The situation grew worse when they brought in a bishop with rank of commander. The chaplain captain and the bishop commander had received information regarding a rebellious Protestant and they were ordered to use their rank to put the battalion of 1,000 men into spiritual order.

Bugles sounded on Thursday, calling Leo's company into formation. They joined with the rest of Leo's battalion, where each soldier was asked to tell of his relationship with the state church and to declare his personal spiritual condition. The men were advised that in order to be good soldiers they must be faithful members of the church.

The bishop spoke of his great interest in the spiritual growth of each serviceman. "You must have your lives right with God. At any time you may be called to go to war and die for your country."

Leo agreed that the idea of having their lives right with God was excellent.

Finally the bishop asked, "How many of you men have never been baptized? Will all those who have been baptized please step over to the edge of the patio in front of the barracks." More than 20 men moved away from their group. The bishop continued, "How many of you have gone for a year without attending Mass?" Many more walked to the edge of the patio.

Leo's company included a young man named Juan Pablo de la Cruz León, a Protestant seminary graduate. Juan knew his Bible well and had tried to humiliate Leo by saying that Adventista preachers are uneducated and poorly prepared for their ministry.

The bishop proceeded with a final statement: "All soldiers will be required to go to confession and participate in Mass next Sunday." Then he added, "I want to see your decision. Will all who plan to comply, please come forward and stand with me."

Everyone moved forward, including the frightened seminarian. Only Leo remained. He stood like a post, willing to face any consequence. Juan Pablo de la Cruz León looked back and saw Leo standing alone. He started to leave the group in front and return to where Leo stood. The bishop saw this and called out, "I'm sorry, soldier. You must stay with the group you've just been with." Juan stayed.

Leo's action perplexed the bishop and chaplain, who wondered, "Why would one man stand in defiance to an order from religious authorities?" They conferred with Leo's captain and lieutenant. They went to the battalion commander, Cardeño Caro. One could almost see sparks flying from the commander's eyes, he became so angry.

FLAGS AT HALF MAST

The bishop, the chaplain, the commander, the captain, and the lieutenant walked to where Leo still stood alone. "Why is it that you refuse to accept the authority of the church?" they asked. "You will see what we are going to do with you."

The military officers walked back to the platform for a final announcement. "There will be no leaves this coming Sunday. Everyone will go to Mass. All will take part in confession and Holy Communion. There will be no exception."

Leo remembered three men standing alone on the Plain of Dura. Christ stood with them in the fiery furnace. Jesus gave Leo courage as he thought, *There will be an exception.*

Lieutenant Salazar, new officer for Leo's section, came and said, "Look, Pinedo. Do you know what they are going to do to you on Sunday? They are going to make you go to confession. They plan to force you to take part in the Mass. If necessary, they will tie you up and carry you there." Leo prayed as Lieutenant Salazar spoke.

"You've got to get out of here early Sunday," the lieutenant continued, "or you will be in worse trouble than now. You must leave early. I will sign a pass. The director for the National College of Women requested a physical education instructor for Sunday morning." He handed Leo a pass.

"Go early and introduce yourself to the college director. Tell her you've been sent in response to her request for someone from my office to come and teach physical fitness. Please stay away all day. If necessary, even hide. The bishop and chaplain, with backing from the commander, are determined to get you to trample your conscience."

Leo accepted the pass with gratitude to God for using the new lieutenant to prepare a way of escape and solve his serious problem.

The director at the National College of Women phoned Lieutenant Salazar after Leo's visit to her school. "We like what Sergeant Pinedo did for our students. Please send him to teach physical fitness every Sunday."

Weeks passed and Leo spotted a new notice on the battalion bulletin board. The major general of the army planned to take 20 brigades on a bivouac for three days. They would leave Friday and return Sunday.

Immediately Leo saw all kinds of Sabbath problems coming out of this. He went to his barracks and fell on his knees asking God to deliver him from this new difficulty. He knew the order from the major general's office would not be changed.

Leo spent the rest of the day fasting. In the evening, he phoned Pastor Hayden and Dr. Potts. "They're going to keep us out all day Sabbath, but I'm not going to do it. With this new commander it may be a matter of life and death for me. I want to live! Can you help?"

With much difficulty, Pastor Hayden and Dr. Potts contacted their friend Commander Flores. "My dear friends," he replied. "I'm very sorry not to be able to do anything at this time. The order came from a higher military command and cannot be changed.

"If it was something to do with my battalion, it would be a delight for me to help. I did promise to help Leo Pinedo, but please understand, I'm not in charge of his battalion any more. Really, there's nothing I can do when an order comes directly from the major general's office."

The missionaries called Leo with regrets for their failure to get him released from the Sabbath bivouac.

Leo continued to fast and pray. "My Dear Father in Heaven, You have promised, 'God is faithful, who will not allow you to be tempted beyond what you are able, but with the temptation will also make the way of escape, that you may be able to bear it. Please help me to believe Your promise. Help me to stand true in honoring Your Sabbath."

Friday morning arrived, with Leo still praying for deliverance. In just one hour his squad was to join with 20 brigades in a march that would keep him out all day Sabbath. *What do I hear? Bells ringing!* Leo looked at his watch. Exactly 11:00 a.m. Bells were ringing across the Republic of Peru, announcing the death of a high government official.

Barracks flags were lowered to half mast. Peru's minister of war was dead of a heart attack. A new order came from the major general of the army: "THE WEEKEND BIVOUAC

IS CANCELLED." Twenty brigades standing ready to march were now asked to send their representative to the government palace to honor the memory of the late minister of war, General de la Puente.

Leo could not rejoice in the death of Peru's minister of war. It was a sad moment; his country went into national mourning. Still, he could not help but be impressed with another promise, "We know that all things work together for good to those who love God" (Rom. 8:28). Leo believed that the Lord permitted this to happen at the precise time when officers were determined to make him march on Sabbath against his conscience.

Friends came and said, "Pinedo, we don't understand. You sure lucked out. Captain Sotillo already told us that he planned to make you carry a pack weighing 50 kilos tomorrow morning. He intended to make sure you broke your Sabbath. Now his plans against you are frustrated.

"But listen, Leo! It won't be long before everyone is laughing at you. You're going to be forced to break the Sabbath you've defended so much."

Back in the barracks at sunset, Leo's knees touched the hard wooden floor. "Thank you, Lord, for making it possible for me to keep another Sabbath." Time after time the Lord helped Leo through apparently impossible situations. Now in just four months he would complete his military service.

A new order for a bivouac came at the end of October. It would last seven days. They would leave on Sunday morning and return the following Saturday, arriving about 9:00 p.m.

Leo thought, *If I go on this one, I'll be marching home all day Sabbath.* He began searching for a way out. If only he could get out of going. *What can I do? My friend Lieutenant Odria is no longer here. Commander Flores has been gone for a long time. How can I be a faithful sergeant and not stay with my squad? There's just no way to avoid this bivouac.*

Before starting, Captain Sotillo approached Leo while he adjusted his backpack and made him take it off. This seemed strange since the captain hadn't checked any other soldiers' pack.

The captain said, "I just want to be sure you have everything packed correctly." Leo thought, *I'm no new recruit. The captain knows perfectly well that everything is in order.*

Captain Sotillo pulled out blankets, sheets, clothes. He threw them to one side. He stopped when a Bible came out. "What's this? Please take this Bible and throw it away. I don't want to see it."

The captain softened just a little and ordered the barracks caretaker to open the door so Leo could go inside and put the Bible away. Leo went inside. With no one watching, he slipped the Bible under his jacket and came back to his squad.

The first night out, the men were to sleep among the hills near La Molina. Before arriving, Captain Sotillo got off his horse and let an aide lead it for him. Somehow the aide wandered down the wrong canyon and became lost.

The upset captain complained, "I'll die of thirst. All my food and water are on that horse. Didn't any of you men see where my aide went?"

Soldiers searched the hills in every direction, trying to find the lost soldier and the captain's horse. When darkness began to fall they finally gave up their search.

Leo listened to some of the men in his squad. "This captain is so cruel that he doesn't deserve any water," they said.

"But we can't treat him like that," Leo replied. "It's true he's made things pretty difficult for some of us. But in no way does this make it right for us to treat him like he treated us."

Another soldier spoke bitterly, "The captain isn't going to have a bed tonight. He won't have a tent. He won't have a place to sleep. We will have the pleasure of watching him die in the cold. And when you think about it, we won't be doing him any harm. Nature will punish him. Tomorrow we can have the satisfaction of digging his grave."

Leo spoke to the young men again. "How can we think this way? Jesus doesn't treat us like that. We must be kind to our captain. Let's go on up the hill the captain told us to climb."

The captain had planned to ride most of the way. He was not in shape for the kind of terrain they struggled over. His heavy boots didn't help, and he got far behind.

Leo and his squad found a cave and set up camp, where they were joined by the rest of their company. After awhile, Leo got out his Bible and began reading from the Psalms. Just then the tired captain walked up, hungry and thirsty, and beginning to feel the cold.

His first words were, "Sergeant, how did you get here with a Bible?"

"Captain Sotillo," Leo replied, "the Bible is very important to me as a Christian. It's more important to me than arms and ammunition are to you."

"OK, OK, it's all right."

"Captain, I'm reading some beautiful psalms that really bring courage to a man when he's tired. Wouldn't you like to hear some?"

Leo read slowly and clearly from Psalm 8: "When I consider Your heavens, the work of Your fingers, the moon and the stars, which You have ordained, what is man that You are mindful of him, and the Son of man that You visit him? For You have made him a little lower than the angels, and You have crowned him with glory and honor. You have made him to have dominion over the works of Your hands." "O Lord, our Lord, how excellent is Your name in all the earth!"

And from Psalm 34: "The angel of the Lord encamps all around those who fear Him, And delivers them. Oh, taste and see that the Lord is good; blessed is the man who trusts in Him!" "The young lions lack and suffer hunger; but those who seek the Lord shall not lack any good thing." "Many are the afflictions of the righteous, But the Lord delivers him out of them all."

Leo moved over and sat down by his captain. "You must be very thirsty," he said. "Why don't you drink some water from my canteen?" Leo shared his food and the two men ate together.

Orders that night called for every man to dig his own fox hole. They would dig 18 or 20 inches in the dirt and sand and make their bed. Everyone must sleep in the same way. Soldiers in Captain Sotillo's company already had decided that they would not share anything with him. If he died in the cold, it would not be their concern. Every man for himself, they figured.

Leo, at least, had support from his squad. He asked a young soldier to help him make a bed. They got everything ready and Leo took his blanket to Captain Sotillo. "Your bed's ready," he announced.

The embarrassed captain replied, "Pinedo, you're a man with a great heart. I didn't think you'd treat me like this after I've done so much damage to you."

"Captain, you deserve better treatment than this."

"Thank you, Pinedo."

Leo helped the captain get covered up with Leo's blanket before he himself walked off into the darkness. He asked a soldier if he would share just a tiny space in his bed where he could sleep. No man in Leo's squad would have said no. He always tried to treat his men in the best possible way. He could ask for a favor and expect to receive it.

Leo awakened early the next morning and decided to make it a day of fasting, asking the Lord to solve his problems for the coming Sabbath. The men marched only a short distance until they came to a sandy place where a water truck waited.

Leo was standing in line to receive his portion of water when Captain Sotillo came up. "Say, Pinedo!" the latter began. "Do you know I dreamed about you last night? Really a mysterious dream!"

"What's it all about, Captain?" Leo asked.

"I dreamed that the commander is going to take you out of my company and put you in the officers' library. We had a terrible discussion and I said he would walk over my dead body before he took you away."

Leo didn't say anything, yet he puzzled over the captain's strange dream.

On Thursday Lieutenant Salazar's horse fell while he rode down a steep mountain side, and broke a leg. The horse was left to die. The officer's own leg pained him so much that he could hardly walk. No emergency vehicle was available to take him to a hospital. Everyone hoped for a car to come and take this man out for proper treatment.

They returned to La Molina on Friday and camped out on a hill. A military maneuver was scheduled for midnight. Leo's assignment involved waking his men at 11:45 and moving them out with their emergency equipment. He watched the setting sun. In moments the Sabbath would begin. The men were already going back to their tents. A field telephone had been placed by Leo's bed. Orders were that when the phone rang he must jump up and complete the mission.

In one final effort, Leo went to Captain Sotillo, hoping for a little sympathy. "Captain, can't you let me off tonight?" he asked.

"I'm sorry, son," Sotillo said.

"But captain, I'm not going out tonight. You can find someone else and get them to do it."

"Sergeant Pinedo! You are going out and if you don't do it in a good way, you will do it by force."

"Captain, my Sabbath is beginning right now. It's a holy day. Please understand that beginning now, I won't be carrying out any secular order."

Leo headed for his tent. *Captain Sotillo is not a man to fool around with. One day he jumped on a man and kicked him until he died. I saw him crush a soldier's skull with a large rock. Recently he turned his horse on a man and he died. What if the captain decides to kill me? No one will lower the flags to half mast just because a soldier died trying to keep the Sabbath.*

Chapter 11

THE CALABOOSE

Lord, I am ready to go with You, both to prison and to death. Luke 22:33.

Leo faced west, watching a sliver of sun still remaining above the horizon. As it slowly sank away, he prayed, "Dear God, help me to keep Your Sabbath banner flying high! Help me to be faithful unto death."

He crawled into his tiny tent, hoping to sleep, only he couldn't sleep. Strange thoughts bounced around in his brain. He remembered how Jacob wrestled with an angel. He thought, *It seems like I'm in a life and death struggle with Satan himself.*

He expected the worst. *Whatever happens will not be good. They'll humiliate me. They'll torture me. They'll make an example out of me. I just wish—I wish I could die—that's the best solution. I'm just an illegitimate son. My parents never seemed to care much about the child of their lust. Well, Father did show concern during the last painful months of his life.*

Thoughts of self pity tormented Leo. *Even the church members. I wonder if they really care? No one from the church has ever come to see me—well, except for Pastor Hayden and Dr. Potts.*

His troubled heart searched for a way out. *Hey, I've got the answer. Right now I can slash my wrists—I'll sacrifice my blood. They won't be able to make me break the Sabbath. Surely suicide is nothing to fear!*

THE CALABOOSE

Leo rolled over on the floor of his tent. *What will happen if I commit suicide tonight? The morning paper will publish a story announcing the death of an Adventista soldier. He committed suicide because he was a coward. This could be a terrible precedent for Adventist youth in Peru.*

Leo realized this could have negative effects for other youth who might want to be faithful to God in the army. The officers dealing with them would say, "Look, you're an Adventista. You're a coward. We had a soldier like you. He simply committed suicide to get out of following an order."

Sergeant Leo Pinedo recognized he'd been thinking wicked thoughts and asked himself, *Why would I lose the kingdom of heaven by committing suicide when I might as well lose it by breaking the Sabbath?*

He determined, *I've got to stop wavering and make a decision. I can take my life and terminate my existence or I can face the consequence of remaining faithful to God. The Lord has delivered me from similar difficulties in the past. I must get these foolish thoughts out of my head. I must give God the opportunity of showing His love for a soldier who wants to honor Jesus and His Sabbath.*

When Pastor Hayden learned Leo would be on a week-long bivouac, he recognized the young man might face the greatest temptations of his life. Immediately he wrote a letter to Leo.

As Leo's mind cleared he recalled words of the letter, which had reached him the day before the bivouac began:

"Dear Brother Leo: When the way is darkest, God is about to give His greatest light. When the path is slippery and difficult, God is ready to give the most help. You must ever go forward. Persecution gives God the opportunity of doing something special for His children.

"Face to face with difficulty, the son of God has confidence in his Creator and reaches for the powerful hand of Christ. Leo, this is the time for you to step forward and take the loving hand of our Lord. He will help you out of the depths. We must go forward even where human limitations would make it impossible."

Leo thought, *The words of pastor Hayden are almost like Christ Himself speaking to me to give me new courage.* A new peace flowed into his heart. He knelt in his tiny tent and prayed, "Lord, I put myself in your hands. If tonight or tomorrow I'm punished, give me patience. If they laugh and ridicule, make me kind. Give me the spirit of pardon for those who might injure me. Lord send your angels to deliver me."

Leo kept right on praying while his fellow soldiers slept. He pleaded with God as though it was the last night of his existence. He talked with Him as though he had never asked another favor in all his life.

In desperation, he found himself saying the same things over and over. He started praying at 7:00 p.m., and at 9:00 p.m. he was still on his knees. The field telephone rang. He said a quick "Amen" and picked up the receiver.

"Hello, this is Sergeant Pinedo."

"Good evening, I'm Major General del Carpio. Tell me, is Captain Sotillo there?"

"General, he may not want to get out of bed. He's sleeping about 20 feet away."

"Sergeant, please do me a favor. Go wake up Captain Sotillo and tell him we just finished a meeting. We've had many activities this past week and the soldiers are worn out. They walked a lot and suffered much. They need to sleep tonight. This is especially true since all the battalions will need to leave at 7:00 a.m. tomorrow for the long march back to headquarters.

"Please tell Captain Sotillo that the group he was to go out with tonight has been cancelled—the emergency operations are called off."

"Yes, General del Carpio. I will give your message to Captain Sotillo immediately."

Leo hung up the phone, crawled out of his tent, and went to awaken Captain Sotillo. "Captain, Captain!" he called.

The weary Captain yawned, "All right, Pinedo, are you ready to go out for our practice?"

"No, it's only nine o'clock!"

"Sergeant, you know our practice operation is scheduled for 11:00 p.m. Why are you waking me up so early? It's been a rough week and I need to get all the sleep I can get!"

"Pardon me, Captain. General del Carpio just phoned."

"And what does he want?" the captain growled.

"Captain, he asked me to advise you that tonight's practice has been cancelled. He's been in a meeting with the leading officers of our division. They decided that the troops need to sleep tonight because they will start out at 7:00 o'clock in the morning in order to reach the barracks by 9:00 or 10:00 p.m."

"It's all right," the Captain said. "Go and sleep now. Tomorrow morning I want to see you with your backpack. We will see what our little Adventista fanatic looks like with 50 kilos on his back."

Leo knew God could take care of Sabbath morning. He hurried to his tent and got on his knees. "Thank you, Lord, for delivering me from taking part in Friday night practice manuevers. I know You will help me keep all 24 hours of this Sabbath."

He thought, *The Lord must have some reason to prove me like this. And those brethren back at the Miraflores church—they've been watching to see what I will do and how the Lord will lead in my life.*

Guess it's kind of important not to let one act of cowardliness destroy all that the Lord's done for me. I must be loyal to my Saviour. I know God will make some way of escape for me in the morning. The enemies of His cause are not going to see me carrying my pack on Sabbath. God will provide a way out of this situation.

With new hope in his heart, Leo fell asleep and didn't waken until 5:00 a.m. He began praying again. The troops were called for breakfast, but he didn't go. There was something much more important than breakfast. All of his convictions regarding the observance of the Sabbath seemed to be in the balance. Leo decided to spend the time in fasting and prayer.

Leo walked over to Lieutenant Salazar and saluted. "Lieutenant," he asked, "do you realize that today is my Sabbath? It will be impossible for me to go back to the barracks with the rest of the men. You can just leave me here. After sundown tonight, I'll figure out some way to get back with all my equipment, even if it means walking all night."

"No," replied the lieutenant. "Do you think a battalion is going to leave a man behind? We will all arrive together alive or we'll all stay behind dead. It's impossible, Pinedo. I understand your situation. I'm just a lieutenant and with my injured leg, I have enough problems of my own. Why don't you talk with the captain? You don't have a thing to lose."

Leo thought he knew exactly what the captain would say, but decided to take the risk anyway. He saluted in good military style. The captain, with sort of a devilish grin, spoke, "I suppose you're coming to me with your little songs about the bad luck that's fallen you today. You were very lucky last night when you got out of the emergency maneuver exercises. Just let me assure you that from here back to the barracks, you will not be getting out of any Sabbath responsibilities."

"Captain, may I just say a word?" Leo moved closer.

"You don't need to speak."

"But I need to talk with you. My dear captain, please let me say a word."

Risking even more, Leo continued, "Captain Sotillo, please, for the love of a young man who has religious convictions. Do you want a man with religious convictions down deep in his heart to be destroyed by his conscience?"

The captain retorted, "I'm tired of all this. Please go somewhere else with all your little speeches." Fearing that Leo might go to the commander, he added, "Go back to your squad and stand by your pack. As soon as you hear the call to march, you will be marching with the rest of the troops. Get going now!"

Leo left, sad and humiliated. *But surely God will do something. I just can't figure out what He is going to do. Oh well, the ways of God are past understanding. My job is to keep trusting!"*

Leo decided on a little plan. *When the captain tells everyone to put on their packs, I will just stand there. The pack will be on the ground along with my other things. The captain will come. Maybe*

THE CALABOOSE

he will kick me or hit me. It doesn't matter if I get a broken bone or two. All my equipment will remain there on the ground.

He kept thinking of the cruelty of his captain. *Maybe he will try and ride over me with his horse. It's more likely that he will tie a rope around my neck and drag me behind his horse.*

Leo prayed, "I'm in Your hands, Lord. May Your will be done."

The six companies in Leo's battalion were to leave at five minute intervals. At the sound of a whistle, each captain would order his company to take their packs and march. Leo faced a most critical moment in his Christian life.

One company left, another, and then a third. The fifth company watched the fourth company move away. Just then they noticed a tremendous cloud of dust. Either a horse or a car was coming. Just as Leo's captain was preparing to call his men to attention, a car arrived. The driver, Señor Castañeda, came from the head army office in Lima.

Captain Sotillo rushed over and said, "Castañeda, I'm sure glad you came with a car. I want you to take Lieutenant Salazar. He has a bad leg. His horse was injured and we don't have another horse. You brought a car out here at a very good time."

Casteneda answered serenely, "Sorry, Captain Sotillo, but I have orders to pick up Sergeant Leo Pinedo. The general in Lima wants to see him."

The poor captain grew pale. He seemed to change colors and then to have seven different colors all at once.

Leo stood in silence—almost reverence. He was practically paralyzed by the words his ears just heard. Leo's companions were surprised and greatly impressed.

The captain walked back a little. "Pinedo, get in that car and go!"

"Thank you, Captain," Leo spoke kindly. He placed his equipment in the trunk of the car and climbed into the front seat. They sped toward the city of Lima, arriving back at the base by 9:00 a.m.

The general waited at the door of army headquarters for a humble son of God as though he waited for some great man. Leo saluted the five-star general.

The general spoke, "How are you, Pinedo?"

"I'm fine, General. Above all, I want to thank you for your kindness in helping me solve my problem in observing the Sabbath."

"You know," the general said, "I stayed awake all night trying to figure out what I could do for you. And I've done something—isn't that right?"

"General, you've done a great deal. I'm extremely thankful to the God of heaven and I trust He will give you His blessing."

"Thank you. I want you to know that Adventist missionary Dr. Clayton Potts from the Good Hope Clinic came to visit me. He asked what I could do and I didn't promise the doctor anything. What I have just done is a very arbitrary action on my part. It's not the way we operate in the army.

"You can't go to your room, because the barracks are locked. You are not to go to church. I suggest you go to the stables and spend your Sabbath there in a quiet way."

"Thank you, General!"

Leo left and went to the stables, where he read the Bible and sang. His voice echoed through the area where they kept the horses. He prayed. "Thank you, Lord, for another miracle. Thank you for impressing Dr. Potts to see the general. Thank you for sending your angel to keep the general awake all night."

Leo never met this general again, but he praised the Lord all during this solitary Sabbath in the stables. He never spent a Sabbath where he felt more reverence for his Creator.

About ten o'clock that evening, troops from Leo's battalion began arriving. Captain Sotillo cursed and swore when he saw Leo.

About three o'clock Sunday afternoon, Leo stood in front of the bulletin board where new orders were posted. The title of one announcement caught his attention. He read, "NEW LIBRARIAN FOR THE BATTALION. By order of the colonel in charge of Brigade B-19 of Santa Catalina, First Sergeant Leo Pinedo is named librarian for his battalion. He is to immediately vacate his present post and begin working in the library."

This was like a time bomb for Captain Hugo Sotillo. Leo stood amazed. *How can this be? Captain Sotillo said after his dream that he would never allow this to happen.*

The colonel who issued the order stopped Leo on the way into the mess hall that evening. "Son, I believe that from now on, no one will bother you. You'll be in the library, where you can read all the books you want. You'll be able to leave on Sabbaths and worship according to your conscience."

Leo thanked the colonel. "This seems too wonderful to be true," he said.

He began his new work as librarian, but the promise of the colonel melted away like a chunk of ice on a warm day. A new order came out totally prohibiting all leaves that were not for specific military missions.

Army chiefs announced the transfer of Captain Hugo Sotillo to a new assignment. He would be replaced by Captain Manuel Sánchez. When the new captain arrived, Leo lost no time in getting acquainted.

"Sir, I'm an Adventista—a member of the Seventh-day Adventist Church. Many times in the past, I've been privileged to attend worship services off base. A new order has made it impossible for me to go recently."

Without further checking, Captain Sánchez said, "It's all right. Go to church as you wish on your Sabbath." He signed a pass and Leo left before sunset on Friday.

Dr. Potts invited Leo home for Sabbath dinner. Before eating, the entire Potts family knelt with Leo and thanked the Lord for what He had been doing and for what He would do in blessing Leo in the final months of his army service.

Leo told them how the major general of the army had sent his private chauffeur to rescue him from the Sabbath march. He told about the kindness of the colonel and how he had been placed in charge of the library. He told how the captain who gave him such a difficult time ever since his induction in the service had been transferred and replaced with a new captain who gave him a pass for this very Sabbath.

Leo left after sundown and hurried back to the base. The colonel who promised he could worship on Sabbath had missed him during the Saturday morning inspection and had gone straight to the new company captain.

"Where's Sergeant Pinedo?" he demanded.

"Colonel, it seems he left and went to town."

"Went to town?" the colonel questioned.

The captain who had signed Leo's pass wanted to impress his colonel. "Who am I to let a soldier go off base on Saturday morning without an official order?" he said. "No soldier can do this in my company and get away with it. He'll be punished severely for this. I'll put him in the *calabosa solitaria* for a month."

The solitary calaboose is a tiny cell with just enough space for one man to stand. From a shower head at the top, cold water can be turned on to torture the prisoner. Three walls are of concrete; the fourth wall consists of a solid steel door with a watertight seal to waist height. Next to capital punishment by firing squad, confinement in this cell, and the attendant tortures, is the worst punishment the Peruvian army offered.

At the end of a blessed Sabbath, Leo walked through the main door into the barracks whistling a happy hymn. A fellow sergeant approached him. "You've had it," he warned. "You're finished!"

Leo reported to his lieutenant and saluted. The lieutenant called him to attention. "About face! Forward march!" When he had completed the commands, Leo stood facing a blackboard with a squad of soldiers on each side.

On the blackboard he read the notice, "When Sergeant Leo Pinedo enters the barracks, he is to be taken directly to the *calabosa*!"

The officer commanded, "Leave your books."

Leo asked for permission to take the books to his room.

"Sorry! Can't you understand the order is immediate? You can put them here on a shelf."

Then the lieutenant relaxed a little, "Do you have the key to your suitcase?"

Leo reached into his pocket and pulled out the key. He was permitted to enter the barracks and put his Bible, Sabbath school quarterly, hymnal, and Morning Watch inside his locked suitcase.

The officer remained silent all the way to the calaboose. He opened the steel door. "Sergeant Pinedo, this is where you'll be staying for the next 30 days."

Leo squeezed into the tiny space. His chin pressed on the hard concrete in front of him. His shoulders rubbed rough concrete walls. He felt cold steel push against his back as the lieutenant shoved the door shut and turned the lock.

Chapter 12

PLUMP AND PRETTY

He who finds a wife finds a good thing, And obtains favor from the Lord. Prov. 18:22.

The concrete box with its steel door pressed tightly around Leo, making it impossible to bend his legs or raise his arms. A coffin would have been more comfortable—he would at least have been in a resting position.

His thoughts drifted off to what his unwed mother had told him about his birth. He thought, *She should have had a girl. They surely wouldn't treat a woman like this.*

He looked back over his life and began repeating words of Job. "Man who is born of woman is of few days and full of trouble.

"He comes forth like a flower and fades away; He flees like a shadow and does not continue" (Job 14:1, 2).

During Leo's time in the army, only two other men had been sentenced to the *calabosa*. Both had died within three weeks. The tension from standing without moving—the impossibility of sleeping—the cold water run over the head at night—it is torture that even very strong men cannot stand for many days.

Questions of life and death left Leo in a quandary. *What's going to happen to me now? The other men died here in the calaboose. If it's the Lord's will, I'm ready to die too. Soon everything will be finished for me and there won't be anyone around to shed tears. I'll be terminated. My time has come.*

He searched his heart and confessed every sin, asking his loving heavenly Father to forgive him. He prayed, "Thank you, Father, for the promise of a resurrection at the coming of Jesus. More than anything else, I want to be ready. Please help me."

His mind focused on reality. *I'm here in the calaboose and I might as well make the best of it.*

The cell contained one luxury—a button near his nose that would ring a bell if he needed to go to the bathroom. Not knowing the time was only 10:00 p.m., he leaned forward and pressed the button with his nose.

In less than a minute a guard came up and shouted, "What do ya want?"

"Sir, I need to use the bathroom."

The guard left and returned with four armed soldiers. Leo didn't understand. He'd been in the army more than a year and a half. He had shown everyone how harmless he was. He never fought with anyone. He never participated in violence. Now they treated him like a violent criminal who might break away or turn on someone at any second. All he wanted to do was go to the bathroom.

Leo walked through the central part of the prison on the way back from the restroom. He saw men who had forged checks, thieves, murderers, homosexuals, drunkards. Each of these men slept on a bed with a mattress, blankets, and a pillow.

Leo compared his situation with the other prisoners and thought, *How can a man like me who has done nothing more than stand up for my religious convictions be treated in such an inhuman way? Human justice? I shouldn't expect more—look how they treated my Saviour. I'm just glad I could honor the Creator by remembering His Sabbath."*

At midnight, a prison guard turned on cold water from the shower nozzle over Leo's head. The water in the cell rose to his waist and he shivered from the cold. He didn't sleep, not even a minute, that first night, or the second, or the third or fourth or any other night in the calaboose.

Friday arrived—Leo's sixth day in the calaboose and the preparation day for the Sabbath. Leo said to himself, *I'm better off than ever. I don't have to ask permission from anyone in order to be able to spend Sabbath in a quiet way. All I have to do is stand quietly in this concrete box with a steel lid. They'll be leaving me here until all my strength is gone.*

As an additional punishment, Leo was taken out at noon to wash the large patio. This area, about 300 by 600 feet, was covered with tile. The midday sun turned the place into an oven. Leo was given a teaspoon. He was to throw out a spoon full of water onto the patio and walk back for more. By the time he returned with the second teaspoonful of water, what he had thrown out the first time had entirely evaporated.

Soldiers walked by and laughed at a sergeant performing a ridiculous and impossible task. When Leo tried to talk with them they refused to answer because the captain had ordered that no one was to speak with him. Some did show some compassion in their eyes—perhaps a certain amount of sympathy. Others walked away shaking their heads and saying, "Poor little soldier."

One friend came when no other men were around. He only whispered, "Pinedo, what are you trying to do anyway? Why are you so terribly interested in keeping this Sabbath day of rest? Why are you living in such a miserable way? They've never punished anyone the way they're punishing you.

"There are men in our military prison for grand larceny, theft, and even murder. They live in luxury compared to you. Don't you think you're a little fanatical about your religion? I think you ought to think seriously about this before you allow the punishment to kill you.

"You could leave your religion for a little while. You'll be out of the army in a few months. Then you can go to your church, keep your Sabbath, and live out your beliefs. You can't keep this up—standing in cold water and going without sleep every night. Your health will be destroyed and you'll be gone. You won't have gained a thing!"

Leo responded quietly, "Friend, thank you for your concern, but please don't worry about me. You don't understand the things that are deep down in my heart. Jesus died on the cross for me. I'm willing to die honoring Him. It's true, I wavered for a while. I've thought everything through carefully and I'm going to be true to my God regardless of the consequences."

The forbidden conversation ended and Leo carried more teaspoons of water. He was back in his cell long before sundown.

On Sabbath morning they took him out of the calaboose and over to the mess hall for breakfast. The officers already knew that Leo would not be taking a teaspoon and throwing water on the patio during Sabbath hours. They knew this soldier would not compromise his convictions, even if they killed him.

They chose to leave him in his cell on Sabbath, but at least they took him out for meals. He was provided special food for breakfast and dinner, and again at supper, but he took some of his food and gave it away. He spent meal time reading a Bible that a friend had managed to hide under the table for him.

While watering the patio on Friday, Leo had managed to make a phone call advising church members that he was in the calaboose. He learned that the church youth would spend Sabbath visiting Inca Union College. In the afternoon they would visit groups of believers along the Rimac River.

Standing alone in his cell, Leo kept thinking about the youth who were sharing their faith. He counted the minutes. "Now, they're in Sabbath school. Now they're having prayer. Will they pray for me here in prison? Someone is giving special music. They're having the mission story. I wish I could be there right now and join them in the Sabbath school lesson."

At around 10:00 a.m. Leo closed his eyes in the darkness of the solitary calaboose. "My Father, why have you abandoned me? Why am I here in this cell? Why am I in a place where I can't even kneel to pray. I don't have a dad. I don't know where my mother is. I don't have any relative to help me and encourage me."

Leo never felt more lonely. He didn't understand his own prayer. He just realized that there was no one to sympathize with him in this tragic prison experience. He didn't even have a girlfriend.

"Lord, if I could only have a sweetheart," he prayed to his heavenly Father. "If you found a Christian girl who is interested in doing missionary work and sent her to this army base, and if she is permitted to visit me, I promise you Lord, I will love this girl all my life. I'll know she's the one you want me to marry. I'll join my life with hers."

By the time Leo finished his long talk with the Lord, it seemed like his heart would break—yet he didn't feel so lonely. He didn't even notice the pain from being cramped in the cruel calaboose.

Armed soldiers came and took him to dinner and again he gave away his food. While he was reading the Bible from under the table, a guard came and said, "Sergeant, they're looking for you. Someone wants to see you in the prison visitors' room."

Leo questioned, "Someone looks for me?"

He wondered, *Who could possibly be looking for me. Could it be some of the young people from the Miraflores church? Maybe the group that was going to the college changed their plans and decided to visit the prison?*

Leo spoke to the guard. "Just leave me here. No one can possibly be looking for me."

As the guard walked away Leo puzzled, *Who would come here to look for me? I'm sure they've made a mistake. The only ones who have ever visited me are Pastor Hayden and Dr. Potts.*

Another guard appeared. "Sergeant Pinedo," he said, "there's a señorita out here and she says she wants to see you."

Leo gulped, "A señorita!" He knew it couldn't be his sister. The last time he heard about her, she was on her way to Aguaytia, deep in the Amazon jungle.

Leo felt very strange deep inside. Not an emotional or sentimental feeling, but a feeling of fear. He remembered his prayer that morning. *I asked God for someone special. Why am I feeling so afraid when God is about to answer my prayer?*

He turned to the guard. "I really think it's a mistake. No one would be looking for me. Why don't you go check to make sure they're not looking for someone else."

The guard returned. "The young lady says she wants to see Sergeant Pinedo. She's a little plump with pink cheeks and she's really pretty."

Leo followed the guard to the prisoners' visiting room. All the way he kept wondering, *Who is this señorita anyway?* Faces of different girls he'd met flashed in his mind. *I told the Lord that if a girl interested in doing missionary work received permission to visit me, I would marry her. Who is this girl that's plump and pretty?*

Chapter 13

GUN OVER THE HEART

If you endure chastening, God deals with you as with sons; . . . But if you are without chastening, . . . then you are illegitimate and not sons. Heb. 12:7, 8.

Leo gasped when the prison guard opened the door to the visitor's room. *Whew! She's really pretty*, he thought. *But why does she have to be so chubby?*

The señorita introduced herself. "I'm Flora Rodríguez Espejo. All the youth from the Miraflores church went to spend the day at Inca Union College."

"Why didn't you go?" Leo asked.

"My cousin phoned yesterday, saying he had just returned from visiting my father in Otuzco. He invited me to come visit his family today. I told him I would. When I realized that his home is not far from the army base, I thought perhaps I should stop by and say hello to the soldier that's in prison for keeping the Sabbath.

"In church this morning, the pastor asked all of us to spend time this afternoon giving out literature. The Lord is coming soon and I really want to share my faith. I've been giving out gospel literature all the way over here.

"I brought you *Vida Feliz* (Happy Life) and *Juventud* (Youth). We heard how you enrolled more than 100 soldiers in the Spanish Voice of Prophecy Bible course so I brought a few more enrollment cards for you to use."

The girl continued, "It's been nice to visit with you and I trust heaven's blessing will be yours. The Lord will give you patience for times of trial like this. The young people are praying that you will be able to return to the Miraflores church soon. May God keep you faithful even unto death."

Without saying another word, Flora turned and left.

Leo's heart pounded away inside his chest. *She seemed shy, but she did all the talking. I hardly said a word. Of course she didn't know about my prayer in the calaboose this morning. And she planned all this before I made my promise to God. This señorita does seem to have a lot of enthusiasm for missionary work.*

The guard hurried Leo back to the calaboose, where he squeezed into the cell as the steel door closed behind him. *Wish it wasn't so dark in here. I could read some of the magazines Flora brought me.*

Leo tried to decide whether to laugh, cry, or be ashamed. He questioned, *Why did this señorita come today?*

He remembered seeing Flora Rodríguez in church, but he certainly had not felt attracted to her. He thought of the other pretty girls from the Miraflores church. *Why didn't one of them come? Why this girl that I haven't even thought about before? Why did I make such a foolish promise to God, that if a girl visited me today I would love her all my life?*

Leo struggled to understand that God really wants to guide youth who desire His will and seek His counsel. Yet he fought with himself, *Why was I so hasty in making a promise like this? Why didn't I wait? What's happening to me, anyway?*

He couldn't comprehend his own reactions. He asked the Lord to pardon his careless thoughts, especially since he prayed that God would show him his future wife in this way. He didn't want the devil to be twisting his thoughts.

He prayed again, "Lord, do help me to get out of this calaboose soon. When I get back to the Miraflores church I'll look for Flora. I'll try to learn more about her. Perhaps someone else will come and take her from me. Then I'll be free from the promise I made."

This last idea brought Leo some satisfaction. *She really isn't that bad looking. Someone will come and save me from this situation.*

His uneasy mind drifted. Almost like an audible voice came the message, "Leo, man only looks at what's in front of his eyes. God looks on the heart."

Leo felt an answer creeping into his mind. *Guess I've been thinking about other beautiful faces. Some of those girls are like dolls, but this is not God's plan for me. The Lord has worked so many miracles. He won't give me just what's left over. He wants to give me the very best. I must leave things in His hand.*

No girl had ever visited him since he entered the army. He became convinced that the señorita's visit could be providential. *When I get out of the service,* he mused, *I will sort of watch Flora for three months. If she doesn't have any other boyfriend and if she's really a Christian, I will consider serious friendship with her. It might even turn out to be a marriage.*

Leo hadn't slept at all for seven days and nights. He felt weary and weak and couldn't trust his own mind. *Why am I wasting time with all these romantic ideas? Why am I dreaming about getting out of the calaboose? I'll be dead before the 30 days are up. None of the others lived more than three weeks. It won't be long now until they'll be turning on the shower over my head and I'll be in cold water up to my waist.*

He felt a bump on the steel door. A key was turning. The heavy door swung open. "Leo, get out of here."

It was the voice of Lieutenant Salazar. "I've been gone for three weeks and I just returned tonight. As I checked the list of prisoners, I discovered your name. You have no business being in here where they put only the most wretched men."

Now Lieutenant Salazar spoke softly. "Take this key to my apartment. Go to my room and sleep. You'll find a mattress, blankets, sheets, and there's soap so you can take a bath. If you need any clothing, socks, or anything, just use mine. Make yourself at home."

Leo listened. "Someone put you here for spite," the officer explained. "Just be sure you leave my apartment by 5:30 in the morning and get back in the calaboose. I've arranged for the guards to lock you in. You must be there when the captain checks prisoners at 6:00 a.m."

Leo slept for the first time since his imprisonment. He thought, *Lieutenant Salazar is just like an angel.* He managed to awake at 5:00 a.m. and hurried back to his cell in order to be there when the captain checked at 6:00.

Since he was a friend of the guards, the lieutenant arranged for them to let Leo out each night and lock him in each morning. Of course, he risked relations with his superiors in doing this.

The captain stopped by every day at 6:00 a.m. to see if Leo was still alive or if he should call men to come and bury him. Since the captain checked personally, the guards felt they were not implicated in this affair.

Leo accepted the kindness of Lieutenant Salazar, recognizing that God could use this officer to save his life. He thanked the Lord over and over for the miracle of the lieutenant coming to his aid.

Under these conditions, he felt blessed to be in the calaboose. At night he enjoyed a good bed, a nice apartment, a beautiful bathroom, and a wonderful hot shower. The barracks were never like this.

When the 30-day prison sentence ended, Leo went and knocked on the door of the captain's office. A voice inside called, "Who's there?"

"Captain, this is Sergeant Pinedo."

A gruff voice replied, "OK, what do you want?"

"Captain, I'd like to visit with you for a minute."

"One minute! All right?"

"Captain, I've completed my 30 days of punishment. Do I get to return to my work in the library or are you going to keep me in the calaboose? I'm awaiting your word."

The captain came over and gave Leo a big *abrazo* or hug. "Pinedo, please forgive me. I did this for spite. I wanted to look good with the colonel. You never deserved this kind of treatment. I signed your Sabbath pass and then I punished you for using it.

"Please take a seat. You've been very useful to us here in the service. You've helped in every way. I've appreciated your spirit of cooperation. You've shown leadership ability as a sergeant and we appreciate the work you've done in the library."

The tough military officer broke down; tears flowed down his leathery face. "I'm, I'm an unjust man—may God punish me. I was sure you were going to die and I did nothing about it."

Leo smiled. "Don't worry, Captain. God took care of me. I'm just very happy that my time in the calaboose is over."

The captain reached for a handkerchief and dried the tears from his face. "Sergeant, how would you like to have a pass so you can go out tonight? Let me give you three passes so you can go see your girlfriend."

Leo imagined the captain had heard about the girl who came to see him during his first Sabbath in the calaboose.

The captain questioned, "Do you have a girlfriend?"

"No, Captain, I wish I did, but I really don't." Leo looked straight into the eyes of his captain, "Could I ask you a special favor?"

"Why, of course. Tell me what you want."

"Sir, instead of giving me passes for three nights, why don't you give me a pass for Sabbath?"

The captain checked his calendar. He wrote down the dates for the next three Sabbaths on three passes. He signed his name and held them out for Leo to take.

"Please forgive me. My pride didn't permit me to cancel the punishment I ordered for you. I knew it was unjust, but pride made me carry it through to the end. I just thank God you didn't die as I was sure you would. I promise I won't be punishing you any more.

"I only wish we had more men in the army with convictions like you. A man who has religious convictions he won't give up for anything is a man of real worth."

Leo stood tall. "Thank you, Captain. It's the Bible that gives men courage to stand up for what's right."

Leo continued his work at the library. It was sort of a refuge for high ranking officers from captain up. Some officers who came to the library actually had been brought to the army base at Santa Catalina for punishment. They were allowed to live with other officers, go to the mess hall, and use the bar and casino and library facilities. They were not permitted to have passes to go off base.

One of these was Major Alayza, from Arequipa. Reports circulated that he tried to kill a colonel, hoping to get his position. Fortunately he failed, but the military punished him because of his intent to kill.

Leo walked by the officers' casino on his way to the library. Major Alayza, who had been drinking too much, made signs for Leo to enter. Like a good soldier, Leo saluted. The major said, "Stop whatever you're doing!"

He held a bottle of whiskey in his hand. "Take a drink! At this very moment I want to drink with my sergeant."

Leo looked at him and said, "Major, you have a very high position in the army. You are much superior to a poor sergeant. You'd degrade yourself by drinking with someone like me."

Major Alayza exploded. "That doesn't interest me. Didn't I tell you, I want to drink with a sergeant?"

"Major, I'll be frank. The truth is I don't drink."

"Oh, now you begin to tell me how things are. I want you to know that here, there is no one who doesn't drink. Do you know who Major Alayza is? I'm here because I almost killed a colonel for the simple reason he was not in harmony with my ideas. I've killed a lot of soldiers and I'm capable of killing a sergeant like you. Either drink with me or I'll kill you!" He reached for his holster and pulled out a pistol.

The drunk major tottered toward Leo with a pistol in his right hand while he held a bottle of whiskey in his left. He shouted, "Either drink or die! I'm ready to kill you right now."

Major Alayza leaned forward and pressed the gun into Leo's ribs just over his heart. "For you to die from the bullet in my pistol is nothing to laugh about. I'll give you a couple of minutes to think about it. You'd be a stupid idiot to die for not drinking. I'm to be respected, understand?"

Leo felt the point of the gun poking between his ribs. "Major Alayza, it's not that I don't respect you. I appreciate all the officers. It's just that I have convictions about taking care of my body and I don't drink. I don't even use caffeine beverages. If I'm punished for not drinking, OK. If you want to kill me for not drinking, that's your problem. Major, you can do what you want. I just want you to understand that I don't drink. I'm not going to drink any of your whiskey."

Leo stood still with the point of the pistol pushing into his chest right over his heart. *All this major needs to do now is tighten his finger on the trigger and I'm dead.*

Chapter 14

WITCH DOCTOR REMEMBERS

That you may become blameless and harmless, children of God without fault in the midst of a crooked and perverse generation, among whom you shine as lights in the world, holding fast the word of life" Phil. 2:15, 16.

Leo grew pale as he felt the pressure and pain from the gun held tightly against his chest, just over his heart. He wondered, *How many more heartbeats until Major Alayza pulls the trigger?*

"Oh, my Father," Leo prayed, "You let the witch doctor cure me when my mother believed her small son would die. You brought me out of the whirlpool and saved me from the boa. I'm just an illegitimate son. You made me your son and transformed a life from lust to love. You've worked miracles to help me keep Your Sabbath here in the army. You kept me from dying in the calaboose. Why do you abandon me now?"

Leo heard what seemed like the voice of the old Serpent himself, "Don't be a fool. You can drink and live. A few swallows of whiskey won't hurt you. You don't have to get drunk to satisfy the major. Just take a little drink."

Another voice echoed in Leo's ears—words of Scripture quoted by Señorita Flora when she visited him during his first Sabbath afternoon in the calaboose. "May God keep you faithful even unto death," and the promise of Jesus in Revelation 2:10: "I will give you the crown of life."

Leo thought, *Lust will lead me to take a drink just to save my life. Love will keep me true to Jesus regardless of the cost.*

Major Alayza growled, "I've waited long enough, I'm going to pull the trigger. You bastard can have what you deserve!"

Suddenly Leo realized he and the major were not alone. Captain Martinez, like a guardian angel, stood with them. The captain gently nudged the major's arm.

The drunk officer spoke: "This shameless sergeant doesn't want to drink with me. He doesn't appreciate me and I'm not one to be disrespected."

The captain replied, "This young man doesn't drink. How are you going to force him to take your whiskey if he doesn't drink?"

"I never asked him if he wants to drink. I simply told him that he has to drink with me."

Captain Martinez grabbed the hand holding the pistol and the gun went off. But the captain had pulled the major's hand so far back that the bullet went flying overhead and not into Leo's heart.

Two years of military service ended and Sergeant Leo Pinedo mustered out with honors. He knew the most important honors were not from his government. The real honor will come when Jesus gives out stars to those who have lived to save souls.

Leo's first interest after leaving the army was to visit the Miraflores church and find the plump and pretty señorita. It didn't take long for him to be convinced that she had no boyfriend. Just to be sure, he determined to watch Flora closely for three months.

His second interest and most important immediate need was to find a job. Every time he told a prospective employer that he couldn't work on Sabbath, they refused to give him work. When he took a job and waited until Friday to tell them he would not be working on Sabbath, they fired him on the spot.

By the end of two months, Leo's small savings from the army was all used up. He had no place to stay. His back ached from sleeping for weeks on park benches and he hardly had food to eat. Yet he felt happy as he walked down the main avenue of Miraflores known as Commandante Espinar.

A honking horn caught his attention. Dr. Clayton Potts drove up to the curb. He talked with Leo, and the upshot of it was that Leo was immediately hired to care for the grounds of the Good Hope Clinic. Then the clinic put him in charge of the laundry. Later the Inca Union Mission requested his services as an office boy, and during the years he worked there he completed high school, graduating from Miraflores Mission Academy.

By the end of three months after his army discharge, Leo had completely assured himself that the plump and pretty young lady at the Miraflores church had no boyfriend. Flora Rodríguez Espejo always carried a hymnal and a Bible, but he never saw her with any fellows.

One evening after Sabbath vespers, he approached her. "Flora," he said, "you're a wonderful Christian girl. Why don't we get better acquainted? I'd like to be your special friend."

She blushed and Leo told himself, *The prison guard was right, she really has pink cheeks.*

Flora tried to overcome the shock. "These are serious things you're talking about. I don't want to rush into anything. Let me pray about this for three months."

Leo's first reaction was to forget about this girl and look for someone else. *I've already waited three months. Anyway, all I asked is for her to be a friend.*

As he thought of the promise he had made to the Lord that lonely Sabbath in the calaboose, he agreed with Flora to wait for three months. They saw each other occasionally, but never went out together. Leo noticed that Flora was an excellent Sabbath school teacher for the children's divisions, and she was always giving Bible studies and distributing literature.

Love grew in Leo's heart, even though he only watched from a distance. Before the second three months were up, he knew he would never want to love anyone else. He believed that God had chosen Flora to be his wife.

When the second three months was up, Leo talked to Flora again. "Señorita, I believe God directs in all the affairs of our lives. I want to be your friend and some day I want to be your husband. You've been thinking and praying about this for three months."

"But Leo, you asked me to pray about being your friend. Now you're talking about being my husband." Flora trembled as she tried to talk.

Leo wanted to take her hand, but she kept her distance. "Flora, let me tell you my story," he said. "I stood there in the calaboose unable to move. Every bone and muscle in my body ached. My chin and shoulders pressed on concrete. The steel door pressed against my back. I prayed, 'Dear Lord, if there is an Adventista girl that you want me to marry, please send her to visit me here in the prison today.'"

Flora seemed more relaxed as Leo continued. "You came, Flora. I didn't like it at first, but now I'm sure God wants me to share my life with you. During our courtship, we must be very careful in our conduct together and do exactly what God wants us to do. Someday, if we get married and have children and God blesses us with a boy, we'll call him Gideon.

"Flora, I just want you to pray with me and ask the Lord to work it out so that when the proper time comes we can get married and enter the Lord's work together. Right now I must finish my education, and it's going to be a while."

Leo looked into Flora's lovely brown eyes. She smiled and took his hand. They bowed their heads and prayed.

Leo struggled almost four years to complete high school. After another year he stood with Flora in front of a large congregation in the Miraflores church. They pledged their love and listened with excitement to the words from Pastor F. C. Webster, "I now pronounce you husband and wife."

Leo leaned over to kiss his bride, "Thank you, God," he prayed, "for giving me the most beautiful wife in the world."

A year later, the happy couple was blessed with a son. They named him Gideon. He was followed by three lovely girls—Anita, Florita, and Sarita.

Five years after their marriage, Leo graduated from the ministerial course at Inca Union College. The family received airplane tickets from the Upper Amazon Mission and flew to the jungle city of Tarapoto.

Leo delighted in beginning his ministerial internship in the very city where he had attended youth congress and where later he was baptized during a colporteur rally. Flora organized the Sabbath school and spent a great deal of time helping young mothers and children. Leo held meetings, visited, and gave Bible studies.

One Sabbath afternoon Leo and Flora went together to visit patients at the Tarapoto Hospital. Near the front offices they saw an old man seated on a stone. The balding gentleman sat slumped over; his tanned face was lined and shriveled, almost like a prune.

Leo walked by and said, "Hello, Grandpa. Good afternoon! Do you know how to read?"

The man protested, "Why do you think I wouldn't know how to read? Of course I can read!"

Leo questioned, "How would you like to have a magazine?"

"Why not?" the old man replied.

Leo handed him a missionary journal. "And when you get through reading it, pass it on to someone else."

"I'll be glad to do that, son. Thank you. I believe I'll like this."

Leo promised, "I'll bring another magazine next week. And by the way, what's your name?"

"My name's Virgilio Izquierdo."

"See you next week."

Leo and Flora walked away. "There's something about that name. Virgilio—Virgilio Izquierdo. Flora! that's the name of the witch doctor who treated me back on the Ucayali River near my birthplace in Contamana."

The next Sabbath, Leo brought Virgilio Izquierdo another magazine. This time he sat down and began talking. "Sir, please tell me, what part of the country are you from?"

"Well, I'm from the area of Contamana."

Leo mentioned the names of his uncles and maternal grandparents.

"I know them very well," the old man said.

"Did you ever know a young woman named Adela?" Leo quizzed.

"You know, there is something I remember very well. A young lady named Adela Sánchez lived with a man named Pinedo. Their 2-year-old son became terribly sick and Adela feared he would die. I lived in Tipishca; my house was on a lake just off the Ucayali River. I worked as a witch doctor, treating the sick. Adela came with José Pinedo and asked for my services. I prayed to the spirits and spit tobacco juice on the boy's body.

"Later I learned that the Pinedo boy got well. Then I didn't hear any more about him. I don't know the boy's name. He must be grown by now."

Leo threw his arms around the old man. "I'm the illegitimate son you've been talking about. You treated me when you were a witch doctor. Now I've come to share words of life with you!"

The old man beamed. Their friendship grew. Leo started Bible studies with Virgilio Izquierdo.

Leo and his family had lived in Tarapoto for more than a year when he received a letter announcing that the youth directors from the Inca Union and Amazon Mission would be conducting a youth camp at Morales, in the jungle near Tarapoto. They invited Leo to join them.

* * *

Leo's army experience had made him an expert at setting up tents. His early life in the jungle had taught him practical lessons valuable in a camp situation. Youth and leaders marveled at his ability to make use of materials that grew wild in the jungle.

All week long, youth campers played and prayed and studied. Each night Leo stood by a blazing campfire and shared chapters from his life—the story you've been reading—the miracle of how God could take an illegitimate son and transform him into a son of God. He loved the promise of Revelation 21:7, "He who overcomes shall inherit all things, and I will be his God and he shall be My son."

A full moon rose over distant foothills of the Andes on Friday evening. The sound of insects filled the Amazon jungle with a world of music. The campfire burned low and Leo spoke softly. He prayed that the Holy Spirit would reach deep into youthful hearts, just as it had touched his own life. He asked the campers to respond, "Do you want to give your heart to Jesus? Have you decided to love and serve Him always? Do you want your Saviour to keep you as a true son and daughter of God?"

Every youth and every staff member responded to the call by standing around the campfire. They sang together,

> I'll be true, precious Jesus, I'll be true.
> I'll be true, precious Jesus, I'll be true.
> There's a race to be run,
> There's a vict'ry to be won.
> Every hour, by Thy power
> I'll be true.
> —*Author Unknown*

After a prayer of consecration Leo announced, "My greatest thrill as a colporteur was learning that people who had purchased books had accepted the message and were baptized. I rejoiced during military service in seeing men study Voice of Prophecy Bible lessons and then join the remnant church. I kept working for Christ during college years and saw three young men go forward in baptism and begin studying for the ministry. Tomorrow will be a special day in my life. The first converts from my work as a ministerial intern will be baptized."

On Sabbath morning many visitors joined the campers for Sabbath school and worship. At the close of the sermon they made their way to the river and sang while candidates prepared for baptism.

Leo helped the first candidate follow the minister to the deepest part of the river. Campers whispered, "Who is this old man with a wrinkled face?"

Chapter 15

LEGITIMATE AT LAST

We are not illegitimate children. John 8:53, NIV. For you are all sons of God through faith in Christ. For as many of you as were baptized into Christ have put on Christ. Gal. 3:26, 27.

The youth director for the Upper Amazon Mission, Pastor Dwight Taylor, raised his hand. "My dear brother Virgilio Izquierdo," he said, "because you have confessed all your sins, because you love Jesus and want to prepare for his soon coming, because you have decided to leave the things of this world and become a son of God, I now baptize you in the name of the Father and of the Son and of the Holy Spirit."

Campers gasped. "Virgilio Izquierdo! That's the witch doctor!" Leo couldn't hold back tears of joy. He threw his arms around the old man as he came up out of the water to live a new life. "Welcome to the family of God!" he exclaimed.

Many others were baptized and invited to join the campers for the last campfire on Sabbath evening. Leo knew the youth would be inspired by the testimonies from these new children of God.

The fire already burned low when the ex-witch doctor's turn came. Bright moon light flowing through tall jungle trees cast deep shadows across Virgilio Izquierdo's face as he began to speak. "For 31 years I communicated with evil spirits and practiced witchcraft. I've personally been responsible for many cruel murders instigated by my black magic.

"Seven years ago my wife began to study the Bible. The spirits told me to destroy it. I hesitated to obey because it was her book. I became curious and began reading the Bible too. In the end, we kept the Bible and I destroyed my books of magic.

"Leo found me and taught me all the important truths of God's Word. My lust for drug concoctions and alcohol caused a desperate struggle. I just thank my heavenly Father for sending the love of Jesus into my life. I can say that through His power the victory has been won and the satanic spell of witchcraft has been broken."

The old man turned to Leo. "It's possible that during the years I served the devil, God entered in a little and helped me do the right thing for you as a toddler. Or perhaps the Lord healed you in spite of what I did.

"I thank God for permitting you to live. I'm glad the Holy Spirit led you to teach me how to love Jesus and to prepare for baptism. I rejoice to be a member of the Seventh-day Adventist Church and to know that Jesus has forgiven all my sins."

Each evening, honor campers lit the fire while their fellow campers sang,

> Oh, set the campfire burning,
> Let's sit around the blaze
> And store some right good memories up
> To use in coming days.

The last campfire ended and only Leo remained to watch glowing embers from what had been a beautiful fire. The revelations of the converted witch doctor touched off memories of his mother—a mother he wanted to love but who never seemed to love him.

I just don't understand, he thought. *How could my mother abandon me? One of the last things my father ever did before his financial world collapsed was to send me back to Contamana to see my mother. I had just turned 17 and hadn't seen her for more than 10 years.*

LEGITIMATE AT LAST

My heart beat fast as I walked to her house. She knew I was coming and planned a big fiesta with family and friends. When she discovered that I didn't drink and didn't smoke or dance and that I was trying to follow the standards of God's Word as practiced by Adventistas, she opened the door and told me to get out of her house.

Adela screamed, "I don't need a son who's left the mother church. You're nothing but a bastard anyway. Get out of here and don't ever use my name again."

Leo understood what she meant. In Spanish-speaking countries children take the surnames of both parents. His full name was Leo Pinedo Sánchez, but she had asked him never to use the name Sánchez again.

These memories of his mother brought tears trickling down Leo's cheeks. When he got out of the army he had looked up his mother. She questioned him:

"Are you still a follower of this fanatical religion?"

Leo answered, "Mother, the religion of the Bible will always be a part of my life."

She started shouting, "You're a devil—get out of here and don't ever come back!"

This hurt Leo more than all the rough treatment he had received in the military. He took his suitcase and hurried to the street, where he opened his Bible in search for comfort. He leafed through the psalms. It was a verse in Isaiah that really popped out at him: "Can a woman forget her nursing child, and not have compassion on the son of her womb? Surely they may forget, yet I will not forget you" Isa. 49:15.

Leo remembered how proud he had been to invite his mother to his wedding. But her first question spoiled it all: "Are you going to get married in an Adventista church?"

"Yes, Mother," Leo replied. "It's the place where Flora and I want to give ourselves to each other and to God."

Adela answered, "Don't expect me to come to your wedding then. I won't dirty my soul by entering a Protestant church."

Leo picked up a stick and stirred what remained of the hot coals from the campfire. Words of the campfire song rang in his ears.

> As sure as stars are shining,
> There'll be a by and by,
> When we'll be looking down the years
> To see with memory's eye—
> A picture of good campers
> With faces all alight,
> Who sat beneath the stars and sang
> Around the campfire bright.

By now the coals were turning black. But there was still the brilliant light of the moon. Leo dreamed of the future. He could hardly imagine that the ex-witch doctor would serve for many years as leader of the little Adventista church at Tocache on the upper Huallaga River. He wondered, *What does God plan for me in the years ahead?*

* * *

God blessed Leo's ministry in the Amazon jungle. Soon church leaders invited him to attend a union session, where they placed hands on him, ordaining him to the gospel ministry.

Eventually he accepted a call to pastor a church in Trujillo in the northern part of Peru.

One day Leo learned that his mother would visit Lima, and he invited her to spend time with his family in Trujillo. "Mother," he said, "my four children want to get acquainted with their grandma."

Adela Sánchez accepted the invitation.

Leo asked his wife and children not to offend her by talking about religion. They took a Catholic Bible and placed it on a small table next to a grapevine loaded with grapes that grew in their patio. Leo suggested, "Let's pray every day that Grandma will pick up the Bible and read it."

They took her to Mass every Sunday. But Leo's mother approached him early one Sabbath morning. "Son," she said, "may I go to your church today and take part in your communion service?"

"Mother, we'll be delighted."

Adela Sánchez attended Sabbath school and church and took part in the ordinance of humility and the Lord's Supper. After Sabbath dinner she surprised her son with another question. "Leo, what would it take for me to be baptized?"

"Mother! that would be wonderful. First of all, you will want to attend a baptismal class in order to understand all the doctrines of God's Word."

Adela continued, "Leo, I've discovered that the Adventista Church is the true church. You see, I've been reading the Catholic Bible that I found on the little table by a grapevine in the patio. The book of Revelation teaches that God's remnant keep all the commandments. Also your home is like a little heaven with Flora and your children. I want some heaven, too."

After attending baptismal class for several months, Leo's mother requested baptism on December 24, her seventy-third birthday.

Leo's four children watched their father lead Grandma into the church baptistry. He raised his hand. "My dear mother," he said, "because you have given your heart to Jesus and asked Him to wash away all your sins, and because you love Him and want to be ready for His coming, I now baptize you in the name of the Father, and of the Son, and of the Holy Spirit. Amen."

After the baptism Adela Sánchez went to the front of the church to give her testimony. "Jesus is very precious. He has forgiven me for so much. I bore a son in lust. My son taught me how to love.

"All my life it's plagued me to know that I'm the mother of an illegitimate son. Somehow the Holy Spirit reached out to Leo and led him to become a son of God. I'm sorry for the way I treated him. I threw him out of my house. I refused to go to his wedding. I told him to never use my name. Today I rejoice to join this pastor son of mine in taking the name of Jesus."

The elderly woman trembled with emotion and fainted away in Leo's arms.

He held her tenderly as she revived. "It's all right, Mother. All the past is gone. Our sins have been made like the snow on the peaks of the Andes." He paused. "Mother, we can praise God. You and I are legitimate at last. I'm the son of a true daughter of God."

Leo turned to the congregation and shared words of Scripture: "Behold what manner of love the Father has bestowed on us, that we should be called children of God" (1 John 3:1); "I will be a Father to you, And you shall be My sons and daughters" (1 John 3:1 and 2 Cor. 6:18).

When Leo arrived as a delegate to a world session of the General Conference of Seventh-day Adventists, he reported to missionary friends that God has blessed his ministry with more than 4,000 persons won for Christ. Since then he has baptized more than 600 others. God has used Leo's hands to baptize thousands of sons and daughters of God. A new joy came to him recently when his sister, Guillermina, was baptized.

Today Leo ministers to children of the *conquistadores* and of the Incas, inviting them to become sons and daughters of God. He has served as pastor of the large Avenida Espana Church in Lima, Peru, and currently is regional director of Adventist Development and Relief Agency (ADRA).